HUNTING EXCELLENCE

THE ART AND SCIENCE OF ACQUIRING THE RIGHT TALENT

VILVA ANTHONY AND **PHYLIS WONG**

HUNTING EXCELLENCE
THE ART AND SCIENCE OF ACQUIRING THE RIGHT TALENT

iUniverse books may be ordered through booksellers or by contacting:

iUniverse
1663 Liberty Drive
Bloomington, IN 47403
www.iuniverse.com
844-349-9409

Because of the dynamic nature of the Internet, any web addresses or links contained in this book may have changed since publication and may no longer be valid. The views expressed in this work are solely those of the author and do not necessarily reflect the views of the publisher, and the publisher hereby disclaims any responsibility for them.

Any people depicted in stock imagery provided by Getty Images are models, and such images are being used for illustrative purposes only.
Certain stock imagery © Getty Images.

ISBN: 978-1-6632-2709-6 (sc)
ISBN: 978-1-6632-2710-2 (e)

Library of Congress Control Number: 2021915534

Print information available on the last page.

iUniverse rev. date: 08/20/2021

CONTENTS

Foreword.. vii

Preface ix

Acknowledgments xi

Introduction... xiii

Chapter 1   Desired Mindset on Talent and Hiring............................ 1
Chapter 2   Business Alignment 9
Chapter 3   Employer Branding..15
Chapter 4   Design Your Hiring Process..19
Chapter 5   Talent-Sourcing 25
Chapter 6   Talent Selection 43
Chapter 7   Hiring Decisions..61
Chapter 8   Integration of New Employees 69

In Closing 73
Appendix A.. 75
Appendix B.. 81
Appendix C.. 83
Appendix D 89
Endnotes/Citations.. 93
About the Authors... 95

FOREWORD

When I was approached by Vilva and Phylis to write the foreword for *Hunting Excellence: The Art and Science of Acquiring the Right Talent*, I felt apprehensive, nervous, but ultimately grateful and honoured to be asked. In the ever-changing world that we are currently living in, where we are all adapting to life in a global pandemic both personally and professionally, Vilva and Phylis provide you with the opportunity to reflect on the basics of how to excel in talent acquisition, talent planning, and ensuring as organizations and business leaders we create the right employee experience.

As a reader they remind you of the importance of the strategies you deploy in attracting, retaining, maintaining, developing, and engaging your employees. How the experience an employee has before, during, and after employment with an organization affects the perception and view of an organization's brand and image.

Having worked in HR for over twenty-five years and experienced the evolution of the role and importance that HR plays in the organization, taking time to pause, reflect, and remind yourself of key principles in businesses core people processes and approach are things we would all benefit from.

Louisa Brady
Global Human Resources Leader

PREFACE

People are the backbone of an organization, and therefore, their skills, knowledge, experience, intellect and personal qualities are highly valuable. Today, organizations are using a variety of terms in describing Human Resources, including "People Experience", "People Operations", "Employee Success" and "Employee Experience". Some still refer to it as "Human Resources". People are instrumental to an organization; they are valuable assets. When you have the right people with the right attitudes in the right jobs at the right time, it tremendously benefits the organization. It helps to create high employee morale and high workplace productivity as well as inspire innovation. In the end, it impacts the bottom line by increasing revenue.

What You Will Gain from Reading this Book

This book provides Business Owners, Leaders, Department Heads, Hiring Managers or anyone involved in hiring, practical and easy-to-apply tips in the space of acquiring the right talents with quick wins. This book serves anyone who has the opportunity to hire at a scale or grow their lines of business, someone who is new to talent acquisition at the mid- to senior levels, and for seasoned talent acquisition professionals who would like to have a ready handbook as a refresher to refer to anytime. The tips described in this book can easily be tweaked to suit the nature of your business and the types of candidates you hire. In fact, all these ideas are helpful tools to ignite some new thoughts when you are working in the hiring space in any season of your business journey. Acquiring the right talent is one of the most fundamental critical processes that relates to the success of the business where it is both an art and a science!

How to Use this Book

This book is intended to be in tips format that makes acquiring the right talent simple and effective, meaning you can refer to any page at any time. Some tips may be applicable to your business for the present moment, and some tips may be applicable to your business in the future.

We wrote this book after taking into consideration different economic climates, ongoing changes of business environments, customer demands, competitions, talent trends, and other related factors.

We hope you enjoy the reading journey.

ACKNOWLEDGMENTS

It is surely a team effort, and we thank our friends and business associates who provided their valuable input along the creative process. We are grateful to Global HR Leader – Louisa Brady for her support and for contributing the foreword to our book. We thank those who offered us their endorsements: Vikram Anand, P. K. Cheng, Gina Yeh, Fazil Fuad, and Boon Peng. Your belief that we have something valuable to share to the world encouraged us even further. We would like to thank the iUniverse Publishing team for supporting us in the journey of editing and publishing our book.

Vilva: This book wouldn't have been possible without the corporate organizations, both SME (small, medium enterprises) and MNC (Multinational Corporations) that provided opportunities for me to experience, develop, and implement insights-related ideas in the Talent Acquisition, Talent Development, and Employee Experience spaces over the last twenty plus years.

I am also immensely grateful to Louisa Brady, Fazil Fuad, and Vikram Anand, who gave me constructive feedback during the final stages of the manuscript. They gave freely of their time to discuss the nuances of the text and encouraged me to explore particular facets of insights that helped us to refine ideas in the book further.

My special thanks to my coauthor, Phylis Wong, whom I truly enjoyed working with on this creative journey. She has been supportive of my writing and ideas. We share an amazing synergy from our like-mindedness, energetic alignment, unwavering support, and by inspiring each other. I look forward to more collaborative projects in the future.

I would like to truly dedicate this book to many wonderful people who have been instrumental in my life. My teenage son, Raagav, inspires me to be a better version of myself all the time, and I wish to be a positive influence on him. I thank my wonderful family and friends, who have always been by my side during every season of my life, for which I am grateful. I would like to thank my amazing work colleagues, business associates, partners, and clients who supported me throughout my corporate career and now as an entrepreneur. My life is enriched by all these awesome people with whom I am grateful to share my life journey.

Phylis: This book would not have been born without past and current challenges, opportunities, and developments provided by my former employers, clients, associates, and coaches. I always appreciate and treasure the journey that we have had.

A special thank you to my two lovely and independent teenage children, Wei Kai and Ling Ya, who always help me in my choice of words, grammar, and computer matters; and my youngest son, Wei Lee, who inspires me to remain curious and to have fun in everything I do.

To Alfred, my awesome husband, your love, care, and patience are the important nutrients in my learning and growing journey in both personal and professional aspects of my life. Thank you for being so supportive, my dear.

Thank you to my parents and siblings for the unconditional support and love all these years. To my friends, thank you for the wonderful friendship and your many sharing that give me different perspectives about life. Everyone and every event of my life are precious gifts to me, that giving me the learning, courage and clarity in doing what I am doing.

I am especially grateful to Vilva, my coauthor. It has been an energized and blessed journey since we decided to write this book together more than a year ago. We have had many meaningful discussions, alignments, realignments along the process. Although we may have different approaches at times, we complement each other so wonderfully. This is possible because we both hold many similar values, beliefs, and purposes in life. Vilva, moving forward, let's together continue to "inspire and co-create to enrich lives".

INTRODUCTION

Have you heard the story of the hare and the hound? Here is our version of the story. One day a strong and powerful hound (dog) was chasing an injured hare (rabbit). After running for a long time, the hound gave up the hunt, and the hare reached her home safely. When the hound returned to his pack, they mocked him, saying that the little one is better than the beast. To this the hound responded, "The hare was going all out as it was running for its life. I was only running for dinner and doing my best."

Do you want an employee who is going all out and performing, or are you satisfied with someone merely doing his or her best, which is mediocre? That could be the fine line between hiring the right talent and hiring a talent!

There are many research studies and statistics that shows hiring the right talent will result in higher productivity, and wrong hires will cost the organization enormously. Here are some key statistics from Mason Stevenson, January 2020:[1]

- The U.S. Department of Labor says the cost of a bad hire can reach up to 30 percent of the employee's first-year earnings.
- The Undercover Recruiter reports bad hires can cost $240,000 in expenses. Those are broken down into costs related to hiring, pay, and retention.
- CareerBuilder says 74 percent of companies who made a poor hire lost an average of $14,900 per poor hire.

Some additional factors that should be taken into consideration of a wrong hire is loss of productivity, negative impact to employee morale and engagement, loss of time and resources to onboarding and training the talent. Therefore, investing your effort and resources in acquiring the right talent is critical to your organization's success.

There are always two sides to a coin as the saying goes. Acquiring the right talent is both an Art and a Science. We will look at facts that support this important process and some soft elements, which we would refer to as human approach to the process. This will provide you with the holistic approach to hiring the right talent.

You and your business can only thrive when you keep learning and evolving as an organization. We describe evolving in this context not just from a technological standpoint but also evolving in processes, including the ways of working, the ways of running a business, go-to market strategy, customer segments, meeting customer needs, changing strategy, cost efficiency, and optimization. This evolution requires a shift in the mindset, without which changes in results cannot happen.

The recruiting world has changed so much, and without doubt, it will continue to evolve. Most of the best practices that we were used to many years ago have either become obsolete or evolved to something better and greater. What you will find in this book are practical ways of how you ought to approach acquiring the right talent into your organization in every season, and you can do it effectively and efficiently.

CHAPTER 1

Desired Mindset on Talent and Hiring

People are not your most important asset. The right people are.
—Jim Collins, *Good to Great*

What Is Your Mindset on Talent?

Talent is the most important asset for any business success. It is even more critical now as talent and technology are key competitive edges and advantages for businesses. Organizations are prioritizing Talent Management by making the right investment in Talent Acquisition, Talent Development and Talent Retention that have become pivotal to the success of businesses.

We propose for you to examine your beliefs on hiring the right talent. Following are some questions that could help you to understand more about your frame of reference on this:

- What does talent mean to you and your organization?
- What are you prepared to do or invest in to get the right talent?
- What fear do you have about hiring the right talent?
- What are potential barriers to hiring the right talent?
- What would help you to hire the right talent?

If you identify any beliefs that are limiting you, we suggest that you tackle them immediately. What you believe becomes your reality. If those are irrelevant or disruptive beliefs in your journey of hiring the right talent, replace them with empowering beliefs.

Here are some examples of common limiting beliefs in relation to hiring the right talent:

- It is exhausting dealing with hiring matters.
- It is difficult to attract talent from large and well-established corporations to join us.
- It is difficult to hire good talent for our industry.
- It is the employer market now, so let the candidate either take it or leave it.
- Our working environment is challenging; therefore, we cannot retain talent.

Your beliefs about talents in your organization determine many of your policies, practices, investments, business decisions, and culture as well as your hiring practices. It is important to self-examine these areas before you read further.

It is definitely a useful energy for you when you have some of the following mindsets or similar thoughts regarding talent:

- Acquiring the right talent is an ongoing process that is worth the organization's effort and investment.
- Getting the right talent is the key job of leaders.
- The organization is as good as who they have.
- Our working environment is challenging; therefore, it is fun and focuses on acquiring talents who enjoy this environment.

What Is the Right Talent?

We will now explore the meaning of what is the right talent. The right talent is not merely having the best qualified person as part of your team. It is all about the right match!

Let us assume, for example, that you are running a local fashion house, hiring the top salesperson from a high-end global luxury fashion house may not be the right match for your business. You should not be aiming to hire only from highly recognized brands or competitors.

Here are some criteria to explore when hiring for the right match:

- Candidates who can perform the job with the skills, knowledge and competencies required.
- Candidates who are motivated to take up the role and highly committed to the responsibilities that comes along with the role.
- Candidates' beliefs, values, and personalities that support the organization's vision, mission, and culture.
- Candidates who demonstrate the ability to synergize with existing team members to achieve common goals.

How Do You Hire for Attitude?

There are many resources highlighting the importance and benefits of hiring for the right attitude, and we advocate this view. You probably wonder, *What are right attitudes? How do you hire for attitude?*

a. **First, what does "attitude" mean?** *Cambridge Dictionary* defines "attitude" as, "the way one think and feels towards something or someone." Whereas the *Oxford Dictionary* defines it as, "a way of thinking, feeling and behaving." In psychology, an attitude refers to a set of emotions, beliefs, and behaviors toward a particular object, person, thing, or event. Attitudes are often the result of experiences or upbringing, and they can have a powerful influence over behaviors (Kendra Cherry, February 2021).[2] Based on these definitions, it truly requires significant effort in getting to know a person's belief, thoughts, and behaviors.

b. **What are the right attitudes?**
Different organizations may value and emphasize different attitudes. For instance, from positive to embraced, responsible, ambitious, humble, interested, determined, self-disciplined, and so on. In order to hire for the right attitude, first decide clearly what attitudes your organization values for now and long-term that ultimately support your vision, mission, and goals.

c. **How do you identify if the candidate has the right attitude?**

From our experience, to hire for the right attitudes it is to use a combination of selection tools such as structured interviews, case studies, situational role plays, and assessments. Do not solely rely on what you hear from the candidates. If you have doubts about their personalities, it is best to clarify your doubts before hiring by applying some of the tools and processes we discuss in this book.

d. **What do you look for in an interview to assess the candidate's personality?**

Even if they are trained or well-prepared candidates, as an interviewer, utilize deep-level listening and observations to see beyond the candidate's answers. Apart from listening to what the person says, it is also how a person says it through eye contact, energy, facial expressions, gestures, hand postures, voice, and intonation. After your series of questions for discussion, study the pattern(s) of the candidate's sharing. Here are some tips in how you could spot incongruence:

- Does the candidate tend to blame others first when something goes wrong?
- Does the candidate act on self-assessment to increase self-awareness when something goes wrong?
- Does the candidate who emphasizes the importance of being positive not take action on things that he or she claims are important due to worries about the future?

Empower Candidates to Make Their Career Decisions

An organization that adopts this mindset would make committed efforts to share with the shortlisted candidates about the good and the fun, while at the same time, the challenges of the role from technical, people, culture, economic, or industry standpoints. When you share authentically about the role, you will help the shortlisted candidate to self-examine if this is the role he or she is interested to pursue. It also gives some perspective where candidates can start thinking about how they can contribute to the organization should they decide to accept the job offer.

Here's an example: John is at the final stage of the selection process for a role of emerging market Development Director. If he is hired, he would inherit a group of sales team members who lacks collaboration and trust among them. It is important for the organization to retain this sales team as they are the pioneers who have close business relationships with the distributors in their respective areas. John should ideally be informed at the outset about this challenge in the team so that he is prepared to lead and drive the change. We propose that you share this information with him before making the job offer.

This may not be feasible to implement in every organization or industry because it involves sharing sensitive organization information. Therefore, find a balance on this approach, and ensure you comply with appropriate policies and regulations.

We would like to stress here that there is no such notion as a perfect organization and perfect candidate. It is all about how much both parties (hiring manager and candidate) understand each other before deciding to join forces. Every individual will have areas to develop, and as a hiring manager, you need to be prepared to face the "imperfection" of a potential hire and allow room for improvement.

Employer and Candidate Assess Each Other

As an employer, you are on a quest to choose the right person for the job. On the other hand, the candidate is scouting for the right career and organization. It is not about whether it's an employee market or employer market. Candidates nowadays are taking the onus on their careers, especially top performers.

An important tip we would like to offer is to treat candidates with respect and sincerity always, whether or not they are the right match for the job. Here are some examples of how you should *not* treat a candidate:

✗ Do not schedule last-minute interview appointments.
✗ Do not make candidates wait for hours or even ten minutes.
✗ Do not neglect to provide updates on application or interview status.

These may seem trivial to some people. However, we have observed how an international brand was unable to recruit good talent that they wanted and ended up with high attrition rates. One of the key factors was that the regional human resource professional and the team demonstrated an attitude of, *We are an international renowned brand, so take it or leave it.* Candidate interviews usually lasted only between five and fifteen minutes. The rationale they gave was that they are good at assessing people and only need five minutes to determine if a candidate is a good fit.

However, after the leader left the organization, hiring the right talent improved, and the company's retention rate increased. The reason was that the new leader instilled the correct mindset in hiring the right talent. You will find more suggested good practices as you read on.

The Importance of the Organization's Culture

It is important to ensure that your organization's environment and culture promote an employee to thrive professionally and have room for growth. Look into the employees' mindsets in current times and in forecasting future trends. Employees are always looking to learn and grow, especially the younger generations who are saturating the workforce.

You can take all the necessary steps in recruiting the right candidate for the job at the right time. However, if your organization's environment does not align with the candidate's values, he or she will feel shortchanged and start seeking other opportunities outside. Let us give you a practical example: a candidate who wants to work in an environment where he or she could innovate as being innovative is one of his or her core values. This innovation could come in the form of products, processes, or tools. However, when the candidate joins the organization, the new employee realizes that the organization does not promote innovation. This is when the new employee would seek opportunities outside the organization as he or she feels limited in expressing innovation creativity.

Key Tip: Ensure that you not only convey the accurate reflection of your organization to the candidate but also assess if the candidate will fit into your organization culture.

Candidate Experience

Organizations are increasingly putting themselves in candidates' shoes, which means that organization are viewing the hiring lifecycle experience through the candidate's lens. "Hiring Lifecycle" is a term used for a complete recruiting process from start to finish. It starts when a requirement for a new employee arises and ends with a new employee onboarded. Each of these stages are explained in detail in the rest of this book so you can fully understand the complete hiring lifecycle.

Now more than ever, candidates' experience is crucial to increase the possibility of desired candidates accepting job offers. Global studies show that when the candidate has positive and engaging experience in the hiring lifecycle process, he or she is more likely to accept the job offer (Resource Solutions, 2020).[3] In the past, it was all about conforming, where organizations set the guideline, rules, and plans and candidates complied. However, as competition for talent tightened and candidates became more skilled, more businesses are looking at everything they do through the lens of candidate experience.

Candidate experience is everything he or she observes, feels, and interacts with as a part of the hiring journey with your organization. The key word here is "engagement." Throughout this book, the ideas and suggestions we provide are in alignment with ensuring a good candidate experience is met from the beginning of the hiring lifecycle until the onboarding of the right talent. This includes engaging all the candidates who are unsuccessful as well. We share more about that process in chapter 7.

Key Tip: Candidates expect a swifter, smoother, more-inclusive recruitment experience that matches their experiences as consumers.

What Are Your Perceptions on Agility and Change?

At the point of this book being written, we are experiencing rapid-paced business climate changes to the global shift that is happening due to the pandemic. Leaders are reevaluating their business priorities, people plans, investments, and the overall business landscape. What we are observing is that those who have been and who will continue to succeed are inevitably those businesses that are agile and that transform their businesses not only to survive but also to thrive. You ought to focus on investing on technology in relation to automation of many of the processes not just pertaining to the hiring process but also to the overall HR process. Look at ways of utilizing tech to make your process as inclusive as possible. Investment in the right automation tools and business processes that will drive your business forward is imperative in the climate we are in right now. Being complacent is a dangerous position to be in. We are living in an ever-changing and agile environment. Seize every opportunity to learn, grow, and change!

One caveat is that too much technology can be overwhelming, especially when systems don't interact with each other properly. When you explore evaluating tools, consult with IT professionals who can help build a seamless array of systems for your business requirement.

Businesses are pivoting toward digitalization more than what we have seen in the past years due to the pandemic, which demands more engagement in the virtual environment. As a result, we are shifting to new ways of working; we cover these aspects in this book as well. Nevertheless, while the world will rebound, we will not go back completely to how things were before. It is worth noting that digitalization and the impact on human behaviors adjusting to these new ways of working will become more evident in the future. Leaders ought to be astute to this shift and determine how they can support the employees in the transformation.

CHAPTER 2

Business Alignment

Great vision without great people is irrelevant.
—Jim Collins, *Good to Great*

Talent Mapping and Talent Planning

While this book focuses on acquiring the right talent, we would like to share an important component that serves as a bridge to the whole hiring lifecycle. What we have seen missing in some organizations is a lack of talent planning that is closely related to mapping talent effectively to available jobs. We explore what this entails in the next few pages.

What Are Talent Planning and Talent-Mapping Process?

It is a business process in identifying the resources required to optimize your business operations connecting to your business goals and, ultimately, affecting your revenue. Do you have a clear talent map of the talents your organization requires to achieve its vision, mission, and goals?

You may wonder, *What is a talent map?* Here is an example that you can easily associate with. It is like a location map. When you want to travel from one point to the other, without the right map, you may be just wasting your time and spending unnecessary effort in getting there even without a clear idea where "there" is! A worse scenario could be you end up at the wrong place after all the effort and time spent. In order to have the right jobs in place for your current and future business, the talent-planning process is critical.

Importance of This Exercise

Why is it important for organizations to undertake this exercise? Here are some of the key reasons:

✓ You require the right jobs in place that will drive your business revenue for now and for the foreseeable future.

✓ Workforce costs typically account to a major part of the business operations cost, and you want to ensure you invest accordingly.

✓ It is an effective way of ensuring people investment is a success and that you have the right numbers of employees with the right skills for the right jobs.

✓ Although this is the most valuable process to undertake before the incorporation of an organization or when organizations go through restructuring or planning for specific projects, this process is often neglected. A famous quote by Benjamin Franklin goes like this: "Failing to plan is planning to fail." where lack of planning can be costly!

Truth vs. Myth

Myth: Talent planning is a complicated process. This is the most common concern we hear from organizations that do not conduct this important exercise. Leaders in organizations further stressed that this exercise takes a lot of their time and effort, and at times, they don't have the resources to do this.

Truth: The process can be a simplified one using a standard form that is easily understandable and convertible to tangible action plans. We have a sample of this template in appendix A, which you can customize to suit your business dynamics and requirements. We would like to encourage you to at least explore doing this exercise and see the value in doing so. If you have a lack of workforce skilled enough to undertake this exercise in your organization, you could always hire an external HR consultant who could conduct this exercise for your organization.

The Approach to Doing This Exercise

In order to have a sustainable talent-planning process, there are three key factors that gel the process together: collaboration + metrics + leadership buy-in. You can find explanations on each of the areas below.

1. **Collaboration**
   - ✓ Seek input from all levels of your organization by using a talent-planning template (refer to appendix A) that your managers can use to gather the information you need to come up with a plan of action.
   - ✓ For greater outcome, the task of talent planning ought to be a collaborative effort between HR and the leadership levels of the organization; that is, Chief Executive Officer to Head of Department to Supervisor.
   - ✓ Work closely with your finance department on budgeting to understand how much your organization can spend on employee costs, including on talent acquisition and development.

2. **Metrics**
   - ✓ You ought to examine past patterns (if any) on how you retain employees to derive accurately an acceptable attrition rate for your organization. One key component to measure attrition rate is to use the industry attrition trend as a benchmark to determine what is acceptable for your organization. This step in the process is important because it can show you how many new hires you will need to make during a certain period regardless of projects. Then once you have determined that rate, you can start to add what new hires you may require based on your goals, giving you a fuller picture of how your talent acquisition strategy needs to be designed.
   - ✓ Assess the current employees' development plan to ensure that they have the abilities to learn and grow in your organization. This activity is usually conducted during the performance review cycle between the managers and employees, which can be done either annually or biannually, depending on the organization's practices.

This shall be an ongoing process so that you are able to capture the latest data.

✓ This analysis will help determine what gaps you have in your current workforce, which can be resolved either by using internal candidates/employees to fill new roles or by hiring externally.

3. **Leadership Buy-In**

✓ If you are the HR leader driving this activity, you would require your leadership buy-in not just to run the initiative but also to ensure the continuation of this process in the future. Talent planning will impact every department in your organization.

✓ Your leaders will be able to assist you to look to the future because they are typically the ones setting the vision and goals. Ask them where they see the business going in three to five years. What new products/services will they want to sell? What gaps in talent do they see right now?

✓ Asking leaders appropriate questions can be impactful to your plan, allowing you to align your talent-planning initiative with the business goals. We have provided a set of questionnaires to help you in this area (appendix B).

Frequency of Talent Planning

Talent planning is best to be completed annually to ensure a consistent approach in managing resources efficiency and identifying development priorities. Once done effectively, this helps tremendously in the recruitment process and in developing your existing talents. By growing your talents, you are building a succession plan and will have incumbents ready for the role when there is a job opening. The talent-planning process fundamentally benefits both segments, Talent Acquisition and Talent Development.

Key Tip: Keep yourself abreast with your country, region, or global talent attraction and retention trends, which you should incorporate in your talent strategy planning.

Organization Vision, Mission, and Values

Do Your Organization's Vision, Mission, and Values Matter?

An organization's vision, mission, and values reflect the organization and its brand in the marketplace. This is an important tool to attract talents whom you desire.

Most often the cream of the crop of talents are not actively seeking jobs; they are more likely focusing on adding value to their existing roles. Hence, how do you attract these talents? Many of these top talents want to make a difference in areas contributing to the world's wellness and to make the world a better place to live in.

Here are some insights about what vision, mission, and value statements are:

- A Vision statement describes what the organization aspires to become in the future. It is a broad and inspirational statement.
- A Mission statement defines how the organization differentiates itself from other organizations in its industry. It is more specific in describing what the organization ought to do now to achieve the vision.
- A Values statement could be referred to as a code of ethics. It defines how people in the organization are expected to behave. It provides a guideline for decision-making.

Following are some questions that can help you to kick-start the thought process around building your organization vision, mission, and value statements.

- What is the purpose of your organization? Why is your organization in existence?
- Who are the people your organization serves?
- What is your organization's core strengths?
- How do you differentiate your products/service in the industry?
- What problems does your organization solve?
- What does solving these problems mean to your organization and its people?
- How are you contributing to society at large?

13

Do you have your organization's compelling vision, mission, and values? If you do not have them in place, it is time to work on this, regardless of your organization's size. You may wish to seek professional advice from experts in this area.

Do Your Employees Embrace Your Organization's Vision, Mission, and Values?

We've observed that some organizations' vision, mission, and values are made as beautiful decoration statements on the walls of their workplaces. It is critically important that your organization's vision, mission, and values are clearly understood and embraced by your people. Your people are your ambassadors, regardless whether they are your front liners, supervisors, managers or department heads. Whenever they are involved in any part of the hiring lifecycle, they can express and demonstrate the live examples toward the organization's vision, mission, and values.

Here is an example. Let's assume one of your organization's value is innovation. During an interview, the candidate highlights an out-of-the box, unconventional ideas of approaching a subject or solving a particular problem. Are your interviewers demonstrating curiosity toward the ideas presented? Do they value innovative thinking? The interviewers can only behave in that manner if they understand, live, and breathe the values of innovation in their lives.

We wish to give you this perspective of your organization having a compelling vision, mission, and value statement because it is an important aspect of an organization's success, not just in hiring the right talent, but also developing and retaining them. It is a powerful strategy in bringing your people in synergy for the common purpose that your organization is driven to achieve.

CHAPTER 3

Employer Branding

Your human talent is your most important talent.

—Carla Harris, *Expect to Win*

Why Employer Branding, and What Is It?

Employer branding is critical in acquiring the right talent from the marketplace. Let's consider this: Why would you as an organization spend money and effort on branding your products or services? Fundamentally, you wish to announce to the world what you have to offer and make your organization known to the industry that you operate in. The same principle applies in employer branding.

We highly recommend that you build your employer brand to attract the right talent fit into your organization. If you do not brand your organization well, you will only attract mediocre candidates, not the best in the market or those who will fit with your culture. When you establish a good employer brand, especially if you are a fairly new organization (maybe an infant in the industry), word of mouth will spread rapidly. In a short time, you will attract candidates applying for jobs in your organization.

We are in a period where more of Gen Z are entering into the workplace.

Key Tip: Young generations, such as Gen Z, are more inspired to work for and stay at an organization they have an emotional connection with. Hence, provide them something to connect with in your organization, the products and services that you deliver; articulate the value your products and services bring to the world.

How Can I Build My Employer Brand?

There are many ways for you to build your employer brand. One of the most effective and proven approaches is use of social media. One of the key purposes of using social media for branding is to build a community and engage your candidates who could be your potential employees in the future. Here are some key social media platforms you could use: Instagram®, Facebook®, YouTube®, Twitter®, and LinkedIn®.

You might ask, "What should I do to brand my organization to potential candidates?" Here are some effective tips that you can implement:

✓ Share stories of employee experiences in your organization through articles, simple video recordings of the employee, stories or videos about events run in your organization, share inspiring stories of candidates' life, what an employee's typical day looks like and short videos of leaders living the organization's values. Align these initiatives to what your organization's values are, which will become your employer value proposition.

✓ One most common question that we have received from organizations is, "This is going to cost me so much. Why do I want to spend my time and effort on this?" Sharing from our personal experience is that using social media platform as your branding model costs less money and effort. Most of these platforms are free unless you wish to use some extra features. But for a start, you could use their existing amazing features for free.

✓ Second, you are not necessarily required to hire a dedicated individual to do this. You can empower your existing employees who are keen to recruit internal employees to support this initiative and create a project team. You will be surprised how many of your employees would volunteer for this as it gives them the pride and joy of working on something exciting—provided you have created a culture of continuous learning and growth. Make your employees your brand ambassadors.

✓ An important tip: Consider injecting a humor element to engage the community at large.

✓ An additional benefit that you will gain while you keep your social media audience engaged is that you can easily post job adverts on these platforms. We discuss this in detail in chapter 5.

Employees as Your Brand Ambassadors

Whether it is formal or informal, offline or virtual (for example, social media platforms, employer review sites), your former and current employees are your possible hiring ambassadors. In the current globalization climate we operate in, information shared is borderless. Employees indeed share about their work lives, emotions, and opinions through social media. Why not leverage on this?

We encourage you to always share your organization's vision, mission, and values to your people. Adopt good practices for employee experiences, and prepare them with necessary information to endorse the organization as explained in the point earlier.

Something you ought to examine before you embark on this journey are your employees' views on your organization. What would they say about working in your organization? Any unhappiness about their employee experiences that they might share will cause negative impact on your hiring journey. We encourage you always to check the pulse of the employees by having regular "organizational health checks" to hear their voices and opinions. This can be conducted via focus group discussions or surveys.

The benefits are twofold. You will get to know your people much better, and you may get surprisingly good input for the organization and its business. Moreover, if there is any negative feedback, you have the opportunity to mitigate it.

When the above is done effectively, you are a step closer to your employees, which will bring many other possible advantages to the organization, such as fostered trust, transparency, effective communication, and high employee engagement.

What Should You Choose to Be If You Want to Attract a Butterfly?

Let's explore this metaphor. If you want to attract a butterfly, first be an attractive flower! If the talents you seek are those with high creativity, those who are passionate, you first need to express that impression to your targeted talent group. You ought to have the supportive practices and policies to support this targeted group of talents, which could be having flexible working hours, allowing working outside the office, mobile workstations at the office, and having clear performance requirements and measurements.

Many years ago, we came across an organization in interior fit-out mega projects. The founder of the organization wanted to hire new team members who were young, dynamic, and creative. Human resources started the hiring efforts. But after months of working on it, they faced challenges. Most shortlisted candidates rejected them during the second and final rounds of the selection process. After analyzing why this was happening, one most obvious reason was after being at the organization two or three times, the candidates observed that the overall conduct of the employees and how things were being carried out, as well as the overall environment, did not match what the organization told them.

The key point to highlight here is to embrace the mindset that it is equally important that your organization impresses your targeted talents through planned efforts. When you do your employer branding right, you emotionally engage with your talents and attract the right talent to your organization.

CHAPTER 4

Design Your Hiring Process

Acquiring the right talent is the most important key to growth.
—Marc Benioff, Founder, Chairman, and co-CEO of Salesforce

It takes a dedicated effort in hiring the right talent. The next key step is designing the process and methods of the entire hiring lifecycle. The planning and process involves:

✓ The study of the requirement and validity of the vacancy/position (hiring need/job analysis). This is referred to as talent planning, which is covered more in detail in chapter 2.
✓ Design and write the job description.
✓ Design the employer branding strategy.
✓ Design the sourcing strategy.
✓ Design the selection strategy.
✓ Design the job-offering strategy.
✓ Design the preboarding strategy.

The design of the sourcing, selection, job-offering, and preboarding strategies will be covered in more detail in the following chapters.

Job Description (JD)

A well-designed and written JD is an important tool to facilitate the whole process of Talent Acquisition, Talent Development, and Talent Retention. You can use it for attracting talent, hiring, training, development, performance management, compensation, career planning, and succession planning. In order to prepare and write a meaningful JD, it is always important to do a thorough talent planning, which you can refer to in chapter 2.

We suggest you include the following information in your JD: job title, job purpose, nature of employment, reporting information, internal role relationships with other departments, external role relationships, responsibilities, competencies, and decision-making authority.

With frequent changes in the industry, technology, and the business environment, we suggest that you conduct periodic reviews on the relevance of your JDs, perhaps on a yearly basis. A sample JD can be found in appendix C.

Transparent Recruitment Process

The overall recruitment process should be treated with fairness and equity. What we mean by this is you ought to ensure the process is transparent within internal employees. For example, if you are considering both internal employees and external candidates for the job openings, keep the internal employees who apply for the job appropriately informed throughout the recruitment cycle. This includes why you reject their applications at the outset, and if they are disqualified along the interview or selection process, inform them why. You could highlight areas of skills or competencies that the employees could develop to be prepared for similar career openings in the future.

Always consider developing your existing workforce, preparing them and promoting them when opportunities arise. Developing your own existing talent base is the most efficient way of managing the workforce. Your organization could develop a robust talent management framework. Alternatively, you could engage external consultants who will be able to assist you in designing and setting up the talent framework aligned to your people and business objectives. Further to the point that we highlighted earlier—candidates seek an organization where they can continuously learn and grow—developing your talent ought to be your organization's key talent agenda.

Compensation Health Check

One of the challenges we have observed in organizations is that compensation equity is somewhat imbalanced between new hires and existing employees. When you hire externally, you tend to be mindful of the market compensation structure to ensure you attract the right talent. However, when compared to your internal employees at the same level and skills or even higher, they may be paid lower than the new hire.

It is imperative that you consistently conduct a "compensation health check," as we like to call it, in which you conduct a review of salary or total compensation benchmarks on an annual basis to ensure you are on par with the market compensation structure. Your total compensation will include salary and bonuses, as well as other benefits including nonmonetary ones such as medical, insurance benefits, education benefits, flexible work arrangements, various leave plans, and holiday incentives. The best practice is to engage the appropriate consulting organizations in the country you operate in to gather and analyze this data. Using the data, evaluate your current compensation strategy, and amend as required to ensure that your internal employees are paid equitably. These are important areas in which you ought to invest.

Diversity and Inclusion

A question you should ask yourself is if you have a diversity and inclusion policy in your organization? You may wonder what are diversity and inclusion. It is having a diverse background of employees and an inclusive workplace that engages all employees. Some of the areas of diversity include culture, race, ethnicity, disability, religious beliefs, generations, gender, and sexual orientation.

Most multinational organizations practice diversity and inclusion in their workplaces. They intentionally create policies that support hiring of diverse individuals. If your recruitment model doesn't include diversity and inclusion as an important talent acquisition pillar, you may be losing in attracting the right resources into your organization, people who could provide the insights and perspectives you require to drive your business forward.

Here are some examples. How many women are on your leadership team? Do you consciously ensure that you hire a specific number of women into leadership positions? Do you reject a candidate because of sexual orientation or even race? These are some great beginning questions to give you a perspective on how you want to drive diversity and inclusion culture in your organization. Establish the appropriate hiring policy and organization values that support an inclusive workplace and target the method of identifying and bringing diverse candidates to your organization.

Key Tip: As an organization, you should intend to drive toward being recognized as an employer choice for employees. Globally, businesses and the workforce are ever evolving, and candidates are seeking employers who encourage and nurture diversity.

Frequent Process Review

Business environments, government policies, economies, and human behaviors are all changing rapidly. What is relevant and effective today may be obsolete tomorrow. It is indeed paramount that organizations review the human resource practices and policies regarding Talent Planning, Employer Branding, Sourcing, Selection, Compensation and Benefits, Diversity and Inclusion, and others on a more regular basis than in the past. Perhaps yearly review is a general average. It is noteworthy that the HR department is a business partner to the organization, so it is vital that HR policies and practices are as dynamic as the organization's business goals.

Some general guidelines in conducting the review include:

- Set clear objectives for the review.
- Set a clear scope of the review.
- Form a task team.
- Determine the frequency of review, and set the date accordingly.
- Decide the methodology to use for the review.
- Tabulate the findings.
- Submit proposed changes for approval.
- Communicate the enhanced policies and practices company-wide.

An important tip: Measure your hiring effectiveness, and use data analytics efficiently. For example, analyze hiring metrics such as the followings:

- Which sourcing channel produces the highest success rate?
- Which selection techniques/assessments produce the highest success rate?
- Quality of hire, employee retention: How long does a new hire remain in employment in your organization? Assess employee engagement index between six and twelve months of new hires joining your organization. Assess new joiner's performance within the first year of joining your organization.
- What is the candidate experience/satisfaction score captured through survey?

Knowing these facts will help you decide how you can refine your hiring strategies and invest the right resources and funding in the right places.

CHAPTER 5

Talent-Sourcing

Time spent on hiring is time well spent.
—Robert Half, Founder of Robert Half Inc.

In this chapter we will share sourcing strategy and sourcing channels. First, let's look at sourcing strategy, which is how you attract or seek the candidates you desire for current or future job openings in your organization. Strategizing your sourcing effectively is critical to the success of the hiring process because this is a key factor in attracting the right talent.

Sourcing Strategy

Hiring Pitch

This could be parked under your employer branding effort. It is crucial to do it right for effective candidate sourcing. Speak to your target audience directly, connect with them emotionally, and articulate sincerely who you are and who you want to hire. Consider your target talents like your customers or target customers.

The high-performing and right candidates would not accept a job offer solely for the monetary compensation. These candidates want to ensure they resonate with the organization's vision, mission, values, and culture before accepting an offer. Simultaneously, your competitors and other employers are searching and approaching the right candidates too. Your well-written hiring pitch will help you stand out and gain the attention of the target talent pool.

Here are some simple and key tips to use in preparing an effective hiring pitch. They can be incorporated with the job advertisement and job description:

✓ You are selling a career, not a job. Present the meaning of the role and what value it brings to the organization.
✓ Explain how the organization approaches career development.
✓ Share the organization's strengths.
✓ Be precise, compelling, transparent, and fun in your hiring pitch.

Key Tip: There is no one approach to having the best written hiring pitch. How you articulate your hiring pitch depends on how you wish to brand yourself to the targeted candidates. The previous tips will help you to formulate the statements.

Proactive Sourcing: What Is It?

Proactive sourcing means that you actively seek the candidates you desire. It is a process of seeking candidates through cold-calling and networking to build an exclusive candidate pipeline in order to attract passive candidates. In this instance, cold-calling means that you call candidates who are in your organization's database, through an online job portal database or contacts you've obtained through your connections. You interview them virtually, most often over the phone.

Passive candidates are those who are not actively looking for a job, but if presented with a job that is interesting, they would be open to explore the opportunity and subsequently to make career move. What you are doing here is primarily hunting for your preferred candidates. This is the most desired approach to building a talent pool in the current economic climate not just for current job openings but also for future job openings.

How to Source Proactively

Here are some ideas for proactive sourcing of candidates. As mentioned in the earlier point, you could gather from your résumé database or records of previous applicants who were stored as KIV (keep in view) if they had not met all your requirements. You could also refer to your previous candidates who were second in line for the hire, but you had a better candidate that fit the profile of that job. These candidates could have gained additional experiences, skills, and knowledge that you might find relevant for the current opportunity.

An interesting fact is that when you reach out proactively to this pool of talents and explore the job opportunity, these candidates will be about four times more responsive to the recruiter/organization outreach.

Talent Pipeline Building: What Is It?

Building talent pipeline means that you gather a pool of candidates who will be ready for hire when the position is available. This is a great approach to having potential candidates lined up for future roles. During this process you focus on gathering resumes and screening candidates primarily over the phone, gathering details about their experiences and skills, current package, expected package, and notice period. You also go through some of the screening process, which we describe in chapter 6.

You will have ready candidates to interview face-to-face or virtually by the hiring manager and hire when the need arises. Working in the corporate world in the talent acquisition space, we have found this approach is evergreen for every hiring season. It speeds up the hiring process and secures the right talent for each role at the right time.

Key Tip: This process will be seamless when your organization has a practice of doing proactive talent planning. You can refer to chapter 2 for more details.

Approach to Talent Pipeline Building

In some organizations, the hiring process could easily take up between one to four months, depending on the skills set required, sourcing approach, sourcing channels, sourcing timeline, interview timeline, and the prerequisite for the candidate to serve the termination notice from their previous employment and join the new organization. The process here extends from the point of advertising or sourcing till having a, "warm body on the seat," which means getting the candidate onboard day 1.

You could build pipeline by either advertising externally using job portals or social media platforms to attract the potential candidates. Another key approach is cold-calling by your recruiters using the various social media platforms such as LinkedIn®, Instagram®, Facebook®, and by using job portals.

> *Key Tip:* You might wonder which roles you ought to proactively build a pipeline, we suggest you focus on skills your business repeatedly recruits for and roles that are hard to find (niche skill set), which are usually quite limited in the marketplace. A key point to remember is that you or the recruiter should not promise candidates that you are hiring for a job now if you do not have an opening at the time. State that you are performing the initial preliminary screening. You obviously don't want to mislead the candidates.

Passive Sourcing: What Is It?

In the earlier points we covered proactive sourcing. For this point, we cover the opposite of it, passive sourcing. This approach essentially means that you initiate the activity of sourcing for candidates once you have a job opening. It is a process of sourcing for candidates typically by placing an advertisement via any channel, running interview events or through referrals. You will eventually wait for interested applicants to apply for the advertised positions. A key point to note is that this type of sourcing will only attract candidates who are actively seeking jobs. You won't be able to tap into candidates who are not out there looking for job opportunities.

You could use this approach if you have only one or a few job openings and are not actively hiring for now or for the future. In some cases, your organization could only be hiring for selected period within a year with small numbers. Hence this approach will suit your requirement.

Proactive vs. Passive Sourcing

We've had questions from leaders who ask why proactive sourcing is better than passive sourcing. In our experience of over twenty years, we have seen that sourcing for passive candidates found most desired candidates the organization wished to hire. You draw out hidden talents who are not actively looking for jobs but fit your job profile and into your organization's culture.

LinkedIn® studies reveal that only 27 percent of employees are actively looking for new opportunities. You might miss the right candidates (73 percent of passive candidates) because you did not reach out to them proactively (Kristina Martic, November, 2017).[4] The key point is that proactively sourcing for candidates is also a way of branding the organization and garner candidates' interest in the organization and the role for which it is hunting talent. This goes hand in hand with your employer branding proposition.

Success of Sourcing Strategy

No two organizations are alike; every organization is unique even though you might be offering a similar product or service as your competitors. As an organization, you always have your own unique branding and product or service portfolio individuality. Hence, the overall sourcing strategy that your organization requires will be different from what another organization requires. Some organizations rely heavily on recruiters; others don't. Some rely on online job boards, some rely on social media, and others prefer networking. Some organizations depend heavily on headhunters. Ultimately, you have the choice to decide which strategy works best for your organization.

Sourcing Channels

More often than not, you'll have to cast a wide net when reaching out to candidates. Let's explore the saying, "Start by fishing where the fishes are." What we are implying here is that don't hold on to one outdated sourcing strategy. Look where your candidates are going, and spend your money there.

The sourcing channel that you might adopt depends on your organization's requirements, the type of positions, your budgetary plan, as well as whether it is for immediate or future demand. In the earlier points on sourcing strategies, we touched on sourcing channels. In this chapter we go more in depth about the various sourcing channels you can adopt that best suit your organization's requirements.

LinkedIn®: Why and When Do You Use This Platform?

Why should you use LinkedIn® as a sourcing channel? Professional networks like LinkedIn® rank as the second most effective sourcing channel for quality hires. LinkedIn® is the most effective channel to use when organizations are interested in finding someone with a certain expertise or experience, or when you need to fill a hard-to-source role. Other uses of this platform include networking, marketing, and engaging with candidates.

One key point you ought to note is that the hires you make via this channel are suited mostly for white-collar jobs. This may not be the most optimal channel for blue-collar jobs. Nevertheless, things are evolving more frequently in the current age, and increasing numbers of blue-collar candidates are using LinkedIn®. Ensure you stay connected with the recent updates in this space. Some of the LinkedIn® features we describe in the next two points are accurate at the time of writing this book. LinkedIn® might alter the features and capabilities, so you ought to keep yourself updated on the changes.

LinkedIn®: Job Posting

Organizations can post job advertisements on their organization's LinkedIn® page. Write a short status summary about the job opportunity, and include a link to the job page from your website to direct potential candidates straight to you. Whoever follows your organization's LinkedIn® page will be able to view this post.

Before you even start posting jobs on your organization's page, we recommend that you engage with candidates and direct traffic to your page to encourage people to follow your organization's page. This is the most imperative step you should undertake. Engaging and networking with candidates takes time and effort, so have patience as you start on this journey.

Alternatively, you can post jobs through a personal profile of probably the recruiter or even the hiring manager. People who are connected with you on LinkedIn®, or is connected to someone who comments on the post, can view the post. It is great to make your post fun and engaging instead of a dry job post. Another creative fact is that you can also post video to promote your job opportunity. These approaches are at no cost to you as you are leveraging the standard free LinkedIn® usage. Whatever you do, kindly ensure you comply with the LinkedIn® usage policy.

LinkedIn®: Additional License for Sourcing and Job Posting

You can also purchase a LinkedIn® license that gives your organization unlimited profile views and database access. Some of the benefits of having this are that you can proactively source for candidates by taking the following steps:

✓ You can reach candidates faster when you expand your searches beyond your personal connections and have wider access to LinkedIn® members. More additional search filter recommendations are made available that allow you to create searches based on ideal candidates you wish to target.
✓ You can contact any candidate via InMail, the LinkedIn® messaging environment, by using customized templates to reach out to candidates quickly and personally.
✓ You can build, track, and manage the candidates you want to hire now or in the future with folders, reminders, and smart to-do lists. There are added features that allow you to streamline your workflow and team activities with shared projects, searches, profiles, and applicant notes.

Internal Mobility: What Is It?

Organizations can make effective use of skill inventories for identifying internal employees for job vacancies. It is a valuable practice to look at internal talent for any vacancy, be it a replacement or newly created roles. Take into account that employee retention ought to be a top priority for any organization. Promoting from within can help you keep your best talents longer. Spotlight open positions during town hall meetings and through virtual communications to your employees. This can be done through e-mails, bulletin boards, internal social media platforms, running competitions, and so on.

When opportunities are provided to internal employees before opening the job for external candidates, it promotes employee retention of highly engaged and committed employees. If you take the proactive approach, which we explained in chapter 2 on "Talent Planning," you can identify the available internal employees for the open position. This is where we discussed futuristic views of any roles in your organization. You develop and build an internal pipeline of candidates who are your employees! One key benefit is you will save on hiring costs when you are able to fill the positions internally, especially senior-level positions in the organization.

Internal Mobility: Communication Guidelines

Communicating effectively is critical for all internal job postings. Transparency and fairness should be explicit throughout the hiring process. The best practice is to ensure that you convey clearly if an employee is unqualified or unsuitable for the role. Refer to the job description as a baseline when explaining the reasons for the rejection of their applications or even why they were not successful in the interviews.

If you have assessments tagged together with the interviews, it will be a supporting tool to build your case. This will eliminate any biasness and ensure fairness throughout the hiring process. We discuss more about assessments in the next chapter.

> *Key Tip:* As a leader, ask yourself how you can continuously support employee growth. Organizations that focus on employee growth as part of their core DNA are more successful than their competitors who do not prioritize employee growth. It is a worthwhile people investment cost!

Interview Events

Let's explore another candidate sourcing channel, the interview event. Typically, this type of event is organized by the organization itself. A walk-in interview event is a fabulous organization branding strategy and also used to attract fresh graduates or candidates who have about two or fewer years of work experience. This approach is widely used to hire mass headcounts for similar roles and to build a future talent pipeline. We have observed this to be an effective sourcing channel and successful if you are a new organization in the marketplace, or if you are initiating a new division within an existing organization. You can run this event either at your organization's premises if the building can cater for large crowds, or at a public venue like a hotel or community hall.

One important factor to note is that organizing an interview event requires the use of a substantial number of resources, effort, money, and planning. We propose you create a project team to work on this. It can take up to a few weeks to months to organize such events depending on your organization's operating speed and your relevant location's regulations or timing required in booking public premises.

An ideal approach would be to advertise prior to the event through all the social media channels. Create hype for the event by announcing door gifts, lucky draw, or any event competition. The competitions can be done virtually prior to the event or during the event itself. We believe that by sharing the above ideas, we might inspire you to explore many different angles.

Job Fairs

Another mass sourcing channel is participating in public job fairs. These types of events are organized by external parties we refer to as job fair organizers. This could be more cost effective as the organizers undertake the advertising and marketing of the event, and there will be less resources, time, and effort involved when compared to an organization-organized walk-in interview event. All you need to do is set up a booth according to the package you choose and assign resources to manage the booth during the event day. The resources should ideally include interviewers, human resource team, and ambassadors who can share their stories to candidates.

One of the key benefits of participating in these job fairs is that it is mostly done virtually and attracts candidates between zero to five years of experience. Again, this is still a good approach to attract candidates for mass hiring for similar roles and to build future talent pipeline. Most organizations take this approach to brand themselves to the candidates in the marketplace, especially those organizations that are new in their respective industry or country.

Key Tip: Approach the organizers about having a speaking slot where you can represent your organization and share wonderful employee stories that will attract candidates to apply to your job openings. These employee stories should be authentic and appealing to your candidate audience.

Graduate Hires: Building Relationships for the Future

Why would you hire fresh graduates? Hiring fresh graduates provides an evenly distributed workforce and promotes an injection of innovation into the organization. It also helps to maintain the cost of the workforce at a manageable rate. You should build relationships with your targeted talent when they are young. There are many ways you can approach this. Start by getting in touch with the future talent at colleges and universities. You may consider Corporate Social Responsibility (CSR) programs and a corporate visit program related to your targeted talent.

Make corporate social responsibility programs part of the organization's ongoing social responsibility to support and collaborate with colleges and universities. One of the activities that you could undertake is running a career day presentation on campus to showcase your company, the business, and the jobs that you offer. Another activity is to teach a particular subject or topic about your industry that is not taught in their syllabus. This will help students gain exposure to your industry, business, and organizational culture.

An example of a corporate visit program is when a fashion house organizes a corporate visit tour of its stores for retail management students each quarter. The intention is to demonstrate the fashion house's history, vision, mission, and values, and perhaps conduct a workshop that supports students in enhancing their knowledge in specific areas.

Both of these ideas are branding strategies to attract future talents into your organization. You provide an opportunity for students to know more about your organization, and there is a high possibility they will apply for jobs in your organization on graduation.

Graduate Hires: Direct Hiring

What we explored on the earlier point is engaging students while they are still studying. Alternatively, if you do not wish to take that approach, you can hire directly, targeting students who have already graduated. Some of the best approaches to hire these graduates are through job fairs, campus on-site recruiting, and online recruiting via social media. It is a great way to attract qualified candidates looking for a job right out of university or college.

Social media platforms can help you attract high-quality graduate candidates. Participating in conversations with them, sharing open positions, and even showcasing your employer brand across your social media platforms can help encourage new grads to apply.

Key Tip: Create a quiz for them to pass the first-level screening, something engaging and fun using a mobile app. These young adults seek an organization they can emotionally relate to, and using unconventional approaches resonates with them.

Intern Hires: Who Are These Talents?

Let's look at another group of talents from universities and colleges who we refer as interns. Interns are students who are required to work in organizations for a certain period as part of their qualifying criteria to graduate. These are students who have not graduated yet. Most of the students are required to complete an internship during their last year of study. However, this varies as universities, colleges, and even countries have different education guidelines. Always verify with the respective universities or colleges in the countries in which your business operates.

Interns are a great source of hire to inject innovation and creative ways of doing things. Interns don't have previous work experience as their frames of reference, so they will do things from a fresh perspective, possibly bringing inspiration to your existing experienced workforce. They are also good resources to work on short-term projects or assignments in your organization. You ought to build a relationship with universities and colleges to attract the right intern talents into your organization. This does take effort, but it can have a good pay-off when done effectively.

Intern Hires: Benefits

The added advantage of having an internship program in your organization is that it can be a great pipeline for finding strong new graduate talent. When interns work in your organization, they are given an inside look at the day-to-day operations of and roles of those employed in your business. You will know if they fit your recruiting demand, and you can offer them full-time positions. What you are doing here is primarily converting them from temporary employment to permanent employment. In a typical hire of an experienced candidate or fresh graduates, you cannot assess work performance prior to the person joining your business. However, it is different with interns. Hiring interns is an approach you can refer to as, "Test first before buying a product or service." You can establish yourself as a leading organization when compared to your competitors because you have the best of the crop!

We have observed that interns who are converted to permanent employment tend to stay longer in the organization provided its values are aligned to their personal values when they joined the organization. From a workforce cost standpoint, it is very efficient as interns are only provided an allowance during their internship period, which is a fraction of what you would pay an experienced employee. There could be different laws about this, so it is best for you to validate on your country laws pertaining this.

Employee Referral: Introduction

Before going external to recruit, it is great practice for organizations to invite their existing employees to encourage friends or relatives to apply for job openings. The candidates could be the employees' friends, their relatives, or someone they know from their acquaintances circle. Be mindful of any internal organization policy that you might have in place that restricts hiring close relatives of employees. In such cases, highlight this so that your employees only recommend relevant individuals.

Benefits of Employee Referral

Employee referral is one of the most cost-effective and efficient sources of recruiting. Many organizations are successful in hiring the right talent using this approach. From our professional experiences, we found that candidates who are hired through employee referral program tend to remain in the organizations longer, hence promoting a high level of motivation and retention. Research also shows that employee referrals are the top source of quality hires in organizations across the globe (LinkedIn® Talent Solutions, 2017).[5]

Hiring through an employee referral program is relatively faster than hiring externally through other channels. Providing monetary rewards to the referring employee of the successful candidate is an effective approach of incentivizing your employees who become partners in building an amazing team within your organization. This monetary reward is only a fraction of what your cost would be if you hired through job portals or through extensive advertising campaign.

Key Tip: The payment condition of the reward should ideally be after the hired candidate is confirmed in his or her employment.

Headhunting

Introduction

Headhunting services have been around for decades. Organizations partner with them, and many consider them as one of their talent acquisition strategies. Due to the cost involved in engaging a headhunter, some organizations are rather cautious in considering such services. However, engaging a high-caliber headhunter can truly bring value beyond the cost involved. When you leverage all the other sourcing channels and balance it with the headhunting service that you deem suitable for the type of role that you are hiring, you can experience efficiency and quality of hire.

When Do You Engage Them?

When do you engage a headhunter, sometimes referred to as employment agencies? Headhunting agencies are engaged to proactively attract employees from other organizations. This channel is best utilized to seek senior-level candidates such as C-suite Executives, Vice Presidents, Directors, or Department Heads to name some of the roles. You could also engage headhunters to source candidates with niche or hard to find skills in the job marketplace. Most often, organizations also use this channel for private and confidential hiring, where they do not wish to advertise the role publicly for various business reasons.

How to Get the Most Value from Them?

To get most value from headhunters, here are some important tips:

✓ First, choose the right one to work with. You need to assess not only the headhunter organization background but also that of the headhunter or consultant who will serve you.
✓ Always understand the coverage of their services in relation to the fees charged and terms and conditions of service. You ought to have clarity about what they will undertake and what is not covered as part of their service.

The following questions and points should be made before engaging them so that you know exactly what their service entails.

1. What is their service fees model, retainer or contingency model?
   • A retainer headhunter organization usually works on an exclusive arrangement with an upfront project commencement fees charged at a certain percentage of the estimated total fees based on an agreed percentage of the annual remuneration. This upfront fee is usually deducted from final billing on placement of the successful candidate.
   • A headhunter organization that works on a contingency basis bills the client only on successful placement of candidate.

- Both approaches involve different commitments from the headhunter organization in the search approaches, selection processes, reporting, and so on.

2. What are the job levels, functions, and industries the headhunter organization specializes in?
   - This is to help you to decide which headhunter organization would be most effective and efficient in fulfilling your talent search requirement.
   - If you are hiring for a human resource director and welcome diversity in human resource experiences, it is wise to use headhunter organizations that serve different industries.
   - If you are hiring for an IT specialist in a certain industry, you may give priority to those who are familiar with the particular industry or that particular role.

3. We recommend that you enquire who are their existing clients or their off-limit organization list. A professional headhunter organization will not "hunt" their existing clients' for you. This may be a concern if the role is niche. This may not be a concern if your industry and the job profile can be sourced from many sources. It is best to engage a headhunter organization who knows your industry or have served a business like yours.

4. Find out the headhunter organization's performance data, such as percentage of searches they complete, the interview-to-offer-to-hire rate, and the percentage of candidates who work for more than two years. You should look for a headhunter organization that closes at least 80 percent of the jobs with high ratio of interview-to-offer-to hire, and placed candidates that work for two years or more.

5. How long does the headhunter organization require to complete a search? Time is money in business; the longer the position is vacant, the higher the opportunity cost to the organization.

6. Make sure you understand the headhunter organization's search methodology. For example, are they using job sites? Online tools? Direct and proactive approach of reaching the targeted talent?

7. Seek to understand the headhunter organization's selection process. For example, do they conduct face-to-face or phone

interviews? What personality assessments do they use—cultural fit assessments, and so on?

8. Assess the headhunter's resourcefulness on his or her interest in serving your organization and keenness in understanding the role and your business. Assess also if the headhunter understands your business challenges and opportunities. Headhunters will represent your organization as an ambassador, so they should have a thorough understanding of these areas to be able to appropriately represent your organization to the candidates they reach out to. Here are some key tips in how you can assess their suitability to work with you:

   - Does the headhunter request a meeting with you, be it face-to-face or virtually?
   - Does the headhunter make a physical or virtual visit to your organization to observe and feel your working environment?
   - Does the headhunter conduct the search assignment, or is the search mainly conducted by an intern or outsourced employee?
   - What challenging jobs have the headhunter handled that demonstrate his or her high level of resourcefulness?
   - Understand how the headhunter prioritizes your assignment.

It is important to work with a headhunter who appropriately represents your organization's value and image. For example, if you are a luxury fashion brand, it is important to work with a headhunter whose image is professionally groomed and appreciative of quality and luxury.

Working Effectively Together on Engaging Their Service

Once you have decided which headhunter you wish to work with, it is important to meet with him or her to explain your organization, business, people, and all information related to the vacancy. You should never assume the headhunter knows everything by just giving a job title or a job description. In fact, an experienced headhunter would inquire deeper to understand the role, responsibilities, and competencies required and personality and cultural fit requirements without merely having an assumption from the job title and job description.

Other discussions may include sensitivity in the marketplace. For example, which candidates or types of candidates should be avoided from the particular talent search. Another important factor to discuss is whether the role is categorized as a private and confidential search, whereby the client's name and brand cannot be mentioned until a later stage of the interview or selection process. Alternatively, if it is an open search, it is ideal to benchmark interviews with your existing selected team members and to find out what successful new hires do differently in their first few months. Work this out clearly with your headhunter on a thorough understanding and agreed timeline for the selection process, parties involved, communication channels, accountability, and so on.

We trust that these tips give you additional information and perspectives for you to leverage the headhunter sourcing channel more efficiently.

Creativity Flow: Sourcing Channel

What we shared earlier are the most effective and common approaches of sourcing strategy and sourcing channels. However, it does not stop you from being creative and exploring other options. Always be unique in how you attract talents. What we suggest is that you don't follow the crowd. Do something different from your competitors. To compete for talents with larger corporations, be it multinational or public-listed organizations with strong branding footings, you ought to stand out. No ideas are outrageous until you implement them.

Here are some additional ideas to ignite your thoughts:

✓ Invite targeted candidates to an event in your organization, such as an opening ceremony or a product/service launch instead of only inviting customers. You not only attract potential candidates but also potential customers!

✓ Collaborate with your clients or business associates in attracting talents through programs such as a test engineers' virtual summit, where organizers provide value like sharing new technologies, products, or latest information. And at the same time, they can announce the job vacancies.

✓ Hire through running a competition. For example, a writing competition to produce the most creative and heart-melting content, where winners will be offered internship or job opportunities.

Key Tip: Measure the success of the sourcing channels by assessing which approach works best for your organization, which approach has the highest return of investment on your hiring cost, and which results in higher retention of the candidates in your organization. All the best in exploring!

CHAPTER 6

Talent Selection

> Hiring the right people takes time, the right
> questions and a healthy dose of curiosity.
> —Richard Branson, founder of the Virgin Group

The next process in the hiring lifecycle is the selection process, when you choose and hire the right candidates. The process includes screening and preselection, interview, assessment, candidate reference checks, candidate background screening, and finally, making the decision to hire. Quite often organizations primarily use the interview as the only main tool for talent selection process. We strongly suggest other proven tools beyond unstructured interviews be used in your talent selection process. In this chapter we discuss some of the tools that are worth considering and to implement where appropriate.

We again highlight that in hiring, we are dealing with people, and everyone and every situation is different. It is important that you apply the process, tools, and suggestions that are relevant to your organization's structure, business model, and requirements. Apply and modify them as required.

Candidate Screening

There are two simple ways to perform candidate screening. The first way is referred to as the résumé screening. It helps to assess if candidates meet the criteria required for the job by going through their résumés. An important tip is to cross-reference their résumés with the job profile or job description to filter out those obviously not qualified. You will generally receive hundreds of résumés for a single job opening. It could be more or less depending on the role, country and job level.

One important factor to consider is whether you could automate this process because it is a time-consuming effort using resources. When you automate this process, you could use system algorithms that highlight key words to filter the résumés. This is accomplished with the software application called the Applicant Tracking System (ATS). You could purchase the app and customize it to suit your business requirements.

After résumés are filtered through, the second approach is performing phone screening. This helps to align expectations between the candidate and employer. During phone screening, the recruiter or hiring manager ought to walk through a checklist that may include topics like pay expectations, full-time or flexible commitment, possible start date, notice period, and other potential deal-breakers. Once you complete this screening, you will have filtered through another layer of candidates you would shortlist for interview.

Candidate Screening: Creative Technology Solution

We would like to propose that you consider using Video Interviewing in the screening process. After you complete your initial résumé screening, you send two to three questions via e-mail to the most promising candidates. You could use some of the questions we have suggested in this book. Candidates then record and submit their answers via a video platform. Thereafter, the recruiting team reviews their recordings and filter further to determine who will move to the next stage of the interview cycle. In order not to compromise the candidate's experiences, recruiters should notify candidates who do not qualify for the next stage.

Here are some benefits you will gain using this technique:

✓ It helps you hire faster as you bring in the right people for the interview.
✓ It gives organizations a better understanding of a candidate's potential such as communication and presentation skills, which you can't assess based on the résumé alone.
✓ You will get ideas on follow-up questions for the formal interview since the initial screening questions have already been answered.
✓ It is cost, resource, and time efficient.

Many reliable software vendors offer this service. You could engage them for cost optimization instead of creating your own system. Many organizations have included this technique in their screening process for some years now, and we are seeing more organizations adopting this approach in the current economic climate. A recent study by LinkedIn® revealed that virtual recruiting is here to stay, and it would be more of a hybrid hiring model that would combine virtual and in-person elements (LinkedIn® Talent Solutions, 2020).[6]

Interviewing

Setting Interview Outcome

Be precise about what outcome you want to get from an interview. For example, if you wish to assess the candidate's motivation in life, ask questions such as:

- What do you look forward to every day?
- What excites you?
- What are you grateful for?

This type of questions are key in ascertaining if the candidates would suit your organization culture, if they are proactive, and their outlooks on life. You don't want to hire a complainer who not only will be inefficient at the job or be inflexible to embrace change but will be a negative influence on others in the organization. Spend some time asking worldview questions to understand and draw out the candidate's personal values. Most interviewers only look at the tasks, and if the candidate possesses the knowledge and skills necessary to perform the job, they don't assess the candidate's attitude or personality. In some cases, interviewers do assess candidate's attitude, but that is not the key determining factor in the hiring decision.

Key Tip: Having recruiting experience for over twenty years, we have come to observe that a candidate's personal values that form his or her attitude is the first determining factor if the candidate is the right fit for the job and the organization. Hiring right means hiring for the right attitude!

Interviewer Mindset

As an interviewer, whether you are the hiring manager or the stakeholder who is on the interview panel, you ought to have an open mindset. The interviewer's mindset is the most important part, and it is usually negligible because many people do not see its significance. Let us give you a few examples. The tendency for human nature is to be attracted to people with the same traits, character, and personality. As a hiring manager, you may be drawn to people who share your values in life or even have the traits that you have. Let's say you are a highly disciplined and organized individual, and when you meet a candidate with the same traits, you tend to resonate with that candidate instantaneously. We are not saying this is wrong. But be mindful to observe this and that you are not biased when it comes to decision-making.

If you are the hiring manager, look for traits in the candidate that are different from yours. When you hire someone who has different personality than you do, it will promote creative thinking and constructive and healthy competition within your team. These are important team dynamics that will help you to innovate and transform the team, something that is critical for the success of any business. Be mindful of your thoughts throughout the hiring process, from the time you place the advertisement, when you screen candidates' résumés, when you interview candidates, and when you make hiring decisions. It is important that you are nonjudgmental even to your own self throughout the process.

Preparation for an Interview

How do you start an interview? What we have seen most is that interviewers tend to be rigid when they start, especially when they are new to interviewing and had little if any training. These tips are easy to follow, and you can practice the day before in front of the mirror at home so that you put yourself in a comfortable state.

It is important to make an effort to put the candidate at ease and relaxed to speak. A person will naturally be less guarded and feel free to speak and reveal himself or herself more openly, thus a more effective and mutual beneficial interview session.

Let's assume you are meeting the candidate face-to-face. Arrange a place for the interview that is clean, quiet, welcoming, fresh, and friendly. Please ensure the front office is well aware of the arrival of the candidate and lead him or her to the prearranged meeting room. Greet your candidate in a friendly and welcoming manner, like a handshake and a smile, and offer a drink. Take into consideration that in some cultures a handshake may not be appropriate, so ensure that you study the candidate's background prior to the interview.

If you are meeting virtually via video conferencing, request the candidate to have the video on so you can see him or her. Greet the candidate and ask if he or she can ensure they will not be interrupted. Invite the candidate to get a drink. As an interviewer, ensure you have a proper background screen, a good sound system, and a clear and good view of you through the camera screen.

Whether it is a face-to-face or virtual interview, ensure your posture is straight, especially when you sit. Don't slouch! As an interviewer, dress decently; be tidy and neat. Dress codes should be aligned to your organization's culture. If your employees don't wear jackets and ties or a three-piece suit, don't wear that type of attire as it won't reflect your organization's true identity. If your employees' dress code is T-shirts and jeans, it is perfectly good to wear that attire. The important factor is that your attire represents the reality of your organization's culture.

Initiating the Interview Conversation

The most frequent question we receive from interviewers is how they can make the interview conversation smooth as opposed to being rigid or intimidating for the candidate. The answer is simple: You merely have a conversation with the candidate as opposed to considering it a question-and-answer session, which we have observed is how most interviewers conduct themselves.

One important factor to consider is how to open conversations. Begin with a warm greeting and welcome. Introduce yourself. Follow with some small talk, which serves as an ice breaker. What do we mean by small talk? It is essentially how you would start a conversation with a stranger. You say, "Hello. How are you doing?" Similar to that approach, you could start with a generic topic, like the weather or travel, and ask the following example questions:

✓ How was your journey to our office?
✓ What do you think about our workspace?
✓ How's the weather been the last few days?
✓ What was a great thing that happened to you this/last week?
✓ Have you been a customer of our company?
✓ If there is something that's happening during that period in the area or country, ask about that.

Key Tip: Avoid political-, religious-, or race-related comments or questions!

Here are some sample questions you can ask if you are interviewing the candidate virtually:

✓ How is the internet connection?
✓ Was it easy to get connected on this platform?
✓ How's the weather there?
✓ What was a great thing that happened to you this/last week?

You notice the questions tend to overlap whether the interview is taking place in person or virtually. Use your judgment about what kinds of questions you can ask the candidate. Prior preparation is always important, so ensure that you are prepared before interviewing any candidate.

Behavior-Related Questions

In addition to task or role-related questions you ask a candidate, we recommend that you ask behavior-related questions. The reason is that behavior-related questions draws out the candidate's personality, view of life, approach to problem-solving or decision-making, relationship skills, negotiation skills, management style, and many more.

These questions will also be useful because you will be able to spot if the candidate shared his or her true experience on the résumé. The fact remains that we often come across many candidates who do not share their true work experiences or accomplishments. Hence, when you ask these questions, you can connect the dots of what is written on their résumés with their responses during the interview. You can also spot congruence or incongruence in their authenticity as a person through their body language, tone of voice, and how they convey their responses.

Here are some powerful behavior-related questions:

✓ What have you done to improve the performance of a low-performing employee?
✓ What is the most difficult business decision you have made?
✓ What is your typical way of dealing with conflict? Give me an example.
✓ Describe a time when you had to use your presentation skills to influence someone's opinion.
✓ There are some boring/mundane/tedious elements of this job. How will you handle the least enjoyable aspects of this position?
✓ What activities excite or energize you?
✓ Who are the influencers in your life? Why are they your influencers?

Key Tip: You can find additional tips on probing for deeper answers from candidates and more behavior- and competency-based interview questions in appendix D.

Questions Not to Ask in Interviews

There are great questions to ask in interviews. And there are also questions that you should not ask in interviews. Do not ask questions such as:

✗ Tell me about yourself.
✗ What are your strengths and weaknesses?
✗ Why are you interested in working for us?
✗ Why should we hire you?

When asked such questions, candidates will likely provide you with technically or what we refer to as professionally correct answers. Their responses will not provide any insight to the candidate's true skills, competencies, or attitudes. Always ask yourself, "What do I want to get out from the interview session with the candidate?" Set the outcome you expect from the candidate, which will help you to formulate the questions that are most relevant for the role, the organization, and you as the manager (if you are the hiring manager).

Earlier in this chapter we addressed certain questions you should not ask or initiate in an interview such as those related to politics, race, or religion. Expanding on that, we now share the following questions that should not be asked in an interview:

×   Are you married or single?
×   Are you pregnant?
×   How many children do you have?
×   What is your race, religion, or ethnicity?
×   What is your gender or sexual orientation?
×   Do you have any disabilities or serious illnesses?

These questions are directly related to the subject of diversity. For the last question on health/disability, you can only ask that question if the job nature is such that it requires someone with certain abilities and in perfect health. Even then you ought to approach the question in a more subtle way, such as asking the candidate, "Are you aware of the ability required to do this job, and will you be able to perform effectively?" In some countries, even this question is illegal, so please do be aware of the respective country's law. Even if there is no law governing such things in the countries that you operate in, it is noble to have humanitarian consciousness when it comes to your perspective of talents, their diverse backgrounds, and their abilities.

We covered diversity and inclusion in chapter 4. First, ensure that you have a clear diversity and inclusion strategy for your organization that promotes the culture of having diversity in your organization's DNA.

Closing an Interview

When you end the interview, it is important to keep in mind the importance of maintaining rapport with the candidate. The reason is that the interview conversation is a platform where you build the relationship. Regardless of whether you feel the candidate is suitable or not for the role, end the session respecting each individual. In life, you just never know who you might meet, when, and whose help you might require in the future. An important factor is to always remember you are representing the organization as an ambassador. The impression you make to the candidate will translate to how the people in the organization conducts themselves.

Thank the candidate for the time he or she has taken for the interview, be it face-to-face or virtually. It is critical to provide the candidate with a time frame for your decision on the hiring. Ensure you follow through promptly as promised, and inform the candidate even if he or she is not qualified to be pursued further in the hiring process. Not informing candidates that they were not successful is a common mistake of most interviewers and organizations. This leaves the candidate speculating and waiting to hear if he or she is going to hear from the organization even though it might take a long time. Don't leave the candidate in the lurch, especially if he or she was not successful in the interview. You want to leave the candidate with a good impression. This relates back to wanting the candidate experience with your organization's hiring process to be a positive one, which we highlighted in chapter 1.

Interview Panel

The interview panel is primarily a group of people who collaborate in the interview process. This group has a stake in the job/role the candidates are being interview for. The interview panel is usually comprised of the hiring manager, human resource representative, department head, or a peer. Depending on the nature of the job, it is best to have a panel conduct the interview to ensure that the selection process is done objectively and to reduce any bias in the hiring decision.

Here is an example of when to use an interview panel. If you wish to interview for an engineer, the interview panel should ideally include the supervisor, department head, project leader, human resources representative, and business stakeholder/partner. You should break the interview into a few stages and assign one to two interview panelists for each stage. We propose for the first stage to assign the hiring manager and a peer.

One of the key advantages of having an interview panel is that you empower the stakeholder in the decision-making, especially individuals the candidate will work closely with in the future. This is a highly advised practice to have in matrix-structured organizations. Do take into account that having an interview panel is time-consuming from the hiring process standpoint. Hence it is best to use this approach for Business-Critical and Leadership roles.

Social Interview

"Social interview" generally refers to a casual interview set up over breakfast, lunch, or coffee. This is another option for you to consider adding to your selection process depending on the level of the position, nature of the position, and your organization's culture. Social interviews can be utilized at any stage of the selection process—early stage, mid-stage, or final stage.

Since it is in a social set-up, it allows both parties, candidate and hiring manager, to converse and seek a deeper understanding on how well they can work together, as well as with the rest of the team members. This is also a good opportunity to observe the candidate's behavior in a social setting. For example, you can observe how the candidate would handle some unexpected inconvenience caused by the waiter or waitress. Is the candidate frustrated, upset? Or is the candidate understanding? It adds a unique perspective of assessing the candidate's response to adversity.

To obtain the results desired from a social interview, it is crucial to set clear objectives, a code of conduct, and evaluation approaches.

Interviewer: Apply the 80/20 Rule

Interviewer shall adopt the practice to apply the 80/20 rule: The candidate does 80 percent of the talking during the interview, and the interviewer does 20 percent of the talking. Most common mistake an interviewer makes is to monopolize the conversation, so the candidate has less opportunities to talk. At the end of the interview, the interviewer likely feels he or she did not get much from the candidate. Which is likely true because the interviewer was doing most of the talking!

Keep in mind that the purpose of the interview is to assess the candidate during this period. An interview usually lasts between a half hour and an hour, and you surely want to get the best possible outcome from the interview. As an interviewer, focus your 20 percent of the talking on the job/role and a little on the organization. Emphasize your organization's unique qualities and development opportunities that separate you from your competitors. Most of your time should ideally be spent asking candidate probing questions.

Key Tip: Allow the candidate the opportunity to ask questions. This is another approach to understanding the keenness of the candidate for the role, his or her interest in the company, and to a certain extent, you can observe the candidate's personality.

Best Conduct of an Interviewer

We have often seen interviewers make mistakes in how they come across to others, especially toward candidates during interview sessions. Another common question we are often asked is, "What is the best way for me to carry myself well as an interviewer?"

Here are some practical and important tips to be implemented:

✓ Be at least ten minutes early, especially when you are doing a virtual interview. Do not try to log into the video conferencing just five minutes before or at the exact time of the interview. You should give yourself time to get connected with the system as sometimes connections may be slow for some reason. When you are having a face-to-face interview as well, be prepared prior to the interview slot. When you as the interviewer show up late for the interview, it leaves a bad impression of you as the leader and for your organization. Candidates see you as the spokesperson for the organization, and if they see you are not punctual, they may assume that your organization does not practice punctuality.

✓ Be polite, considerate, and an active listener. Let us give you an example. When candidates are talking about their work experiences, you find that you want to probe deeper on a statement they said. It is a natural tendency to rehearse in your mind a question or answer. However, the best interview etiquette is to wait until they complete their answer and then ask them the questions you intended. Do not interrupt them when they are talking as you might stop their train of thoughts.

✓ Another important factor is to stay positive and neutral at all times. You may come across a situation where a candidate is saying something negative about his or her situation. Even though it seems justifiable, do not get sucked into those stories and start sharing your view. If you find that what the candidate is sharing is irrelevant for the interview, tactfully steer the conversation in a direction that you wish. For example, ask about any positive learning that came from the experience.

Interviewing is an art and not just based on facts alone. This art surely can be learned by anyone through experience and observation, as long as one is keen to learn. When you master this art, you will be able to tell if a candidate will be a good fit for the job and the organization. This instinct—or what the masses call gut feeling—is based on years of experience. It is not something that can be systematically replicated.

Key Tip: This is an added skill to have when it comes to choosing the right candidates. Everyone who is in tune with their inner selves can harness this wonderful gift every human being possesses. You ought to have the faith that you are intuitive, and trust it at all times. In our endeavor to educate and coach individuals, we have found that our intuition has always been our guiding principle in accurately assessing the situation or the person.

Assessments

Truth vs. Myth

Myth: Formal assessment is not required and is only nice to have. This is the most common concern we hear from organizations that do not conduct any kind of assessment and rely solely on unstructured interview sessions. Sometimes leaders in organizations feel that having an assessment process is time-consuming and at times costly.

Truth: A full assessment may be expensive, but it will save considerable time interviewing candidates who are potentially not suited for the role. When you factor the cost in the time and effort of the whole hiring lifecycle, the cost of an assessment will be a small fraction of the total hiring cost. Assessments aid in filtering candidates from the outset. Combining interviews with these assessment tools will support you to hire the right talent for the role. We propose that assessment be included as part of the interview process.

Tools

Here are some assessment tools to explore and what they entail.

✓ *Personality Profiling:* Personality assessment tools are used to understand the natural tendency of the candidates' personalities. This can also be used for team personality matching and synergy. There are about 2,500 types of personality profiling assessment tools in the market. Please do your due diligence before deciding which one to use.

✓ *Competency Profiling:* We encourage you to apply this tool for your talent acquisition as well as other talent functions, such as talent development. Generally, this is an assessment of a person's competency and behavior toward a role. There are some reputable assessment tools for this; it is a worthy investment for your talent acquisition strategy.

✓ *Ability Test:* This assessment tool is designed to find out specific skills and abilities of a candidate. For example, if analytical skill is crucial to a role, you may engage a proven third-party assessment on analytical skill for your shortlisted candidates.

Case Study

Another assessment best practice is to have candidates do a case study or solve a real problem during the interview. You could get them to present his or her results during the interview by asking the candidate to do a formal presentation. Provide some time and tools for the candidate to do this. This can be done on the day of interview. The quality of a candidate's work is usually easy to compare with that of other applicants, adding an important data point to the final decision, especially when done spontaneously.

Sometimes we might hire the wrong candidate for the role based on his or her résumé and responses during interview. But when it comes to actual work deliverables, some may be incompetent and will fail. This irony is something employers face in the workplace. Hence, implementing a case study as part of your selection approach is powerful when used to assess the candidate's knowledge and technical competencies.

What we have shared here is only an example. Depending on your business nature, instead of presentations, you could use other case study mechanisms suited to your business and roles that you hire for.

Candidate Background Screening

Candidate background screening is a pre-employment check of employment history and validating the work behavior of the candidate. This is a pertinent step that ought to be taken before deciding on the candidate you wish to hire for the role. It is done prior to extending a verbal offer. Some organizations will go the extra mile in not just conducting employment screening but will include a criminal check, an identity check, education check, and/or a credit history check (for specific roles). It is a critical process every organization should ideally adopt and will support the selection criteria and employability decision of the respective candidate.

Reference Check: What Is It, and Why Do It?

Reference checks are part of the background screening process all organizations ought to perform for all their hires. The reference check validates employment history and work behavior of the candidate. One of the primary reasons we conduct reference checks is to avoid hiring candidates who have not been truthful on their résumés or during interviews in relation to the work-related information they provided.

We have seen many organizations in various countries that fall into this trap of hiring candidates based only on their résumés and interview performances. After hiring these candidates, the organization discovers that some of them lied or created fake employment details. Without doubt, you can take legal action on the candidates when appropriate, but you would have loss time, effort, resources, and money in the process of hiring such candidates.

First Step

Request a candidate to provide at least two references from previous leaders they worked with or business partners who supervised them or were responsible for assessing the candidate's performance. Being specific about the references you require will avoid candidates providing references who are their friends or acquaintances and may not provide the results employers seek, which is to validate true work behavior. These individuals may be biased in providing feedback on the candidates concerned. When a candidate is unable to provide these types of references, you can request contacts from their colleagues or even their clients (if that is legally permissible in the country you operate in).

If you are hiring graduates, request that they provide contact information for their lecturers or faculty staff who can validate the graduate's behavior, conduct, and overall performance in the university or college. Some graduates might already have reference letters prepared. Validate them as well to ensure their authenticity.

Calling References

Reference checks are usually conducted by phone and in some rare cases, through e-mail. Here are some best practices you could adopt when calling a reference source:

✓ Identify yourself, state your job title, organization name, and inform them that you are calling about a reference for a candidate you are considering to hire.

✓ Ask if now is a good time to talk or if it would be better to schedule a call for a later time. Always respect the person's time.

✓ Before proceeding further, clearly state that you have the candidate's consent to contact them and that all responses will remain confidential. Responses should not be shared with the candidates regardless of the outcome.

Briefing Reference Sources

When the reference source has agreed and is ready to converse, it is important to begin by giving a brief description of the role for which the candidate is being considered. This helps assure the responses are made in context of that position. Thereafter, ask the questions based on what information you have. Then fill in the information on to the form. It is critical to note that you should clarify any responses if you are not sure about what you heard. People sometimes talk fast, and you may not capture all the points.

Here are some example questions to ask:

✓ How would you describe his or her attitude and motivation toward the work? Please cite an example.

✓ How was the person's enthusiasm and energy?

✓ What was his or her major contribution to the organization?

✓ Would you consider rehiring him or her? If yes, why? If not, why?

Key Tips: Give them time to answer your questions. Do not interject or phrase words for them, especially when they are silent for some time. You are aiming to obtain their comments, so let them formulate them in their own words and sentences. Once you complete asking all the intended questions, thank them for their time and feedback.

Who Should Do It?

Who should conduct the reference check? Ideally, the recruiter or hiring manager conducts reference checks. For senior roles such as C-Suite Executives, Department Heads, Vice Presidents, Directors, and so on, it is more appropriate for the hiring manager to call the references. If the candidate search was undertaken by a headhunter, he or she would conduct the reference check. You can request the headhunter to follow your format (if you have one) or tell them what kind of feedback you expect.

Detailed Background Screening: Introduction

As we shared previously, some organizations will conduct additional screening that may include criminal checks, identity checks, education checks, or credit history checks. Deciding whether you should engage a third-party vendor to conduct a detailed candidate screening would be based on the nature of the job, the job-level seniority, and the level of security imposed on the job. In other words, you can take this approach for high-security jobs or for senior leader positions. For example, positions that require working on national security–related projects or confidential projects. In some instances, for example positions that handle highly sensitive confidential financial information, the organization would conduct credit checks.

Key Tip: You will gain optimum results when you factor in this analysis while you prepare talent-mapping or talent-planning. That process assists you in setting this criteria upfront. Then when you prepare the job description or job profile, you can highlight that these are additional background screenings required for those specific roles.

Engaging Vendors

If your organization is keen to go through the detailed candidate screening procedure, you should ideally engage a qualified legal vendor/provider to avoid any legal dispute. Please be mindful of the fact that in order for your organization to even assign the work to the vendor, you should first get written consent from the candidates, giving their approvals for the background screening. In some countries this may not be a legal requirement. However, the best practice is to obtain written approval from candidates regardless of the law as a matter of ethics.

It is interesting to note that the laws governing candidate background screening differ between countries and even states within the countries. It is sound to always check with a knowledgeable local attorney on this as laws may change over the years.

Key Tip: There are many local country-based and regional-based vendors who provide this service. You can easily locate them by searching online or connecting with your organization's attorney who might have relevant vendors they can recommend. If you are sourcing these vendors online, make sure to verify their credibility in relation to the services they offer.

CHAPTER 7

Hiring Decisions

Making good decisions is a crucial skill at every level.
—Peter Drucker, Mgmt. Consultant and Author

Introduction

The final stage in the selection process is choosing the candidate with the greatest future potential for your organization. To hire right, your focus is to find the person who will add value and bring success to your business. Hiring the right talent means that you not only hire for the right competencies, skills, and knowledge but also for the right attitude. However, we have encountered many employers who solely focused on hiring to fill a position. Beware of such a trap in your hiring journey.

Candidates are unique individuals. Each responds to situations differently, and they can sometimes be unpredictable. Having all the metrics and assessments does not mean you have made the right hire. However, person-to-person communication, which is the face-to-face or virtual interview process, will support you in the selection process.

In an earlier chapter we shared with you the selection techniques and tools to use, including interviews and assessments that you can adopt. Hence your hiring decisions are best made based on a combination of data and a humanistic approach. In practice, this means that you set a predefined criteria on which each candidate is assessed during the selection process. This step supports an unbiased hiring decision. You choose the best candidate and extend the job offer. If and when the offer is accepted by the candidate, an employment contract is drawn up and signed by both parties.

Managing Your Filters and Biases that Affect the Hiring Decisions

We now discuss in more detail about being more mindful of hiring biasness. Hiring biases happen because we are all humans and have our own filters due to our life experiences and preferences. Hiring biases can be costly as they may cause you to hire a wrong candidate or miss a good one. Biases can be positive or negative. For example, whether an interviewer is favoring graduates from overseas or dislikes graduates from overseas may cause some negative effects on the hiring fairness and effectiveness because of the interviewer's prejudice.

Hiring biases, just like other life biases, can be unconscious. Unconscious biases exist in the way we think, feel, and act, but we are not aware of them and how they affect perceptions, information processing, listening, attention, and decision-making.

To minimize biases, first be aware of and acknowledge your biases. Here are some common possible cognitive bias scenarios in hiring:

- Overconfidence bias
  Hiring managers have told us that "With my many years of dealing with candidates and hiring, in fewer than five minutes of interviewing, I will know if a candidate can perform efficiently in the job." This is a possible overconfidence bias of the hiring manager.

- Framing bias
  The interviewer decides how information or options should be presented to him or her. This could cause favoritism toward candidates who can speak fluently or do a better job in presentation. This will be considered favoritism if the job does not require someone to speak fluently or great in presentations.

- Anchoring bias
  Let us say, for example, a hiring manager interviews an excellent candidate and wants to proceed to the next level. However, the candidate decides not to proceed. The interviewer continues to interview other candidates. However, the interviewer rejects candidates who meet the requirements but are not as good as the first candidate.

In this instance, the interviewer is using the first candidate as the subsequent reference point in choosing the right candidate for the role instead of focusing on the original intended requirements for the role.

- Confirmation bias

  For example, an interviewer has heard many success stories about how "ABC Organization" develops top-performing talents. Therefore, when the interviewer interviews applicants from ABC Organization, he or she focuses on getting information that supports his or her opinion that ABC Organization produces top performers, and easily ignores contrary information or signals.

- Halo effect bias

  This happen when an interviewer likes one aspect of the candidate and assessment on other aspects of the candidate are influenced by the aspect the interviewer likes. For example, a candidate has won a difficult project in the market. Due to the halo effect, the interviewer may view all other competencies of the candidate as equally strong. However, winning a difficult project does not equate to having high team spirit, being effective in communication, and so on. The halo effect also happens regarding appearance and outlook, in which the interviewer sometimes tends to associate being well-groomed and having a smart outlook with high performance capability.

- Horns effect bias

  Horns effect is the opposite of the halo effect. It is bias toward a candidate based on one negative aspect of the candidate. For example, some interviewers tend to disqualify candidates who are less attractive on outlook. An interviewer may also score a candidate low in all areas of evaluation due to the fact that he or she did not win a prominent project in town.

Once you become aware of and acknowledge possible biases, utilize the techniques and tools we recommend in this book: clear talent map, job descriptions, interview process, behavior-based interviews, panel interviews, proven assessments and tests, reference checks, background screening, and so on. This provides an avenue for objective hiring decisions for you and your organization.

Managing Unsuccessful Candidates

Informing unsuccessful candidates is part of the process in the hiring lifecycle. It is important to perform this step as equally professionally as all other parts of the hiring process. The key benefit of undertaking this process is to ensure the candidate has a good overall experience in the hiring, which we highlighted as candidate experience in chapter 1. It is also a good practice when the candidates can move forward to their next plan once they are aware of your decision.

How you manage this process varies depending on the vacancies and the level of the selection process the candidates are in. For example, for candidates who are not shortlisted from the online job application, perhaps you could use standard e-mail to inform the candidates. Some organizations address this step in the beginning. In the job advertisement, they state that "Only shortlisted candidates will be notified." You could work on automating this process, which is more efficient. Wherever possible, we encourage you to send a professional e-mail by addressing the applicants' names to inform them by e-mail that their applications were unsuccessful.

For the applicants who go through interviews and subsequent selection process, we suggest that either the human resources representative or the hiring manager contact the candidates to inform them about the outcome and to thank the candidates for their interest, effort, and time. Below are some tips on how to communicate the message professionally:

- The appropriate approach is to give the candidates a call. If text or e-mail is the best communication channel for whatever reason, personalize the message by addressing him or her by name.
- Whether the communication channel is through phone or e-mail, it is always important to do it in a timely manner. Some organizations wait until a successful candidate is offered or hired to inform the unsuccessful candidates. This sometimes takes many months. Our

recommendation is as soon as you decide someone is not the right match for the job, inform him or her immediately.

- Be sincere and courteous; thank all applicants.
- Be authentic when sharing honest feedback for the reasons the person is not selected by using the sandwich method. First mention what the candidate did well in the overall selection process. Follow by sharing the areas where the person did not match the job profile requirements, and if appropriate, offer suggestions on how to work around it. Finally, give some encouragement and wishing the individual well in his or her job search.
- If the candidates have further questions, always respond politely.
- It is also good practice to ask for the candidates' feedback on their job application experiences.

Hiring: A Creative Twist

One pleasant way of inducting a candidate into your organization is to invite the candidate's family or spouse for a lunch, dinner, or tea to create an informal setting of getting acquainted. This is a best practice for senior leaders who you hire into your organization. In some cases, organizations may take this approach even before extending the offer, while others wait until they have extended the offer. It is entirely up to you how you wish to approach this. This is a good global industry practice for both local and expatriate hires.

There are various benefits to this practice. It helps to build a relationship with the candidate from the onset and to create better understanding with the candidate and family. It is also a useful approach to assess the candidate from a different perspective as you can get to know the candidate on a more personal level.

A key factor for the candidate's success in the job depends on the spouse and or family support. Having this informal setting with the superior helps to make the candidate's acclimation into the organization more seamless. It is worth noting that you can adopt this practice if it supports your organization's culture and values as well as your country's culture.

The Employment Offer: Essentials

Here are some important questions you ought to ask yourself about making an employment offer:

- How will the offer be made?
- Who shall be assigned to call the successful candidate to make the employment offer?
- Will the initial offer be extended by text message, via the phone, or by e-mail?

We have observed situations in which the right candidates declined the offer due to how the offer process was handled. One example was when a sales associate decided not to accept an offer after much consideration mainly due to how the offer was handled. When the human resource assistant called the candidate to extend the offer, it was more of an "instructional call" to come and collect the offer letter. The tone and the manner of that human resource person made the candidate rethink whether this was the environment and people with whom he wanted to work.

Another example of this is when a junior recruiter was requested to extend an employment offer to a senior leader/executive, which was done via phone. The recruiter was unprofessional in her conduct, and that made the candidate question the values of an organization that did not undertake this process professionally. Eventually the candidate rejected the offer. This may seem like trivial matters, but these small details may make or break a candidate's acceptance of a job offer.

In previous chapters we highlighted the fact that anyone representing the organization is an ambassador of that organization. It is important that the employment offer is handled professionally. What we mean by that is to ensure the person—whether it is the recruiter, hiring manager, or others—are trained to execute the offer process efficiently. When designing this process, consider the employment offer channel, the tools used, scripts or choice of words, the emotion and tone used when speaking, and so on.

Contract of Employment

Once you extend the verbal offer with the necessary details, you should send the written contract of employment to the selected candidate. This important document is an agreement between the employer and the employee. It is imperative to get legal advice if you are doing it for the first time to ensure you have the necessary clauses to cover both parties. It is a legal binding document, so ensure that it is prepared by a legally qualified professional. In some cases, you may require the employment contract be altered based on certain benefits aligned to certain jobs.

Key Tip: It is a good best practice to review your employment contract terms and conditions periodically to ensure that you are abiding by the employment law in the respective state and country in which you operate.

Understanding and Adhering to Employment Law

Employment law governs the relationship between employer and employees. Different countries adopt different practices of employment law. It is important that your organization and its leaders have an understanding of the employment law in the locations in which you operate. This information is usually available on the country's governing authorities' websites. If you have any doubts, always check with relevant local authorities. In some countries, private agencies provide advice and support relating to employment law to employers for a fee.

By adhering to the employment law, an organization is not only complying in providing a fair and safe workplace, it also reflects on the organization's good image and impression as an employer to the employees, potential employees, and the general public.

CHAPTER 8

Integration of New Employees

You can dream, create, design and build the most wonderful place in the world ... but it requires people to make the dream a reality.

—Walt Disney

Preboarding

Once an offer is made and accepted, the right candidate has been hired, and it is done! Is it true that the hiring process is complete? No, the process does not end there.

This next phase in the hiring lifecycle is crucial. Before a new hire's first day, it is a best practice to ensure that he or she gets acclimated early on with the organization, people, and culture. This process is referred to as preboarding. Your organization should initiate this process when the candidate accepts the job offer, and it continues right through to the new hire's first working day. The focus is to prepare your new hire and drum up some excitement as their first day approaches. Preboarding helps to curb any uncertainty or anxiousness a new hire might feel. This process can also solidify the new employee's commitment to your organization. Be mindful to keep up the excitement that you are igniting in the new hire even after he or she comes onboard. It is indeed an ongoing process. We will look at more details in the upcoming points.

Logistics Preparation

Preboarding logistics arrangements ought to be handled before the new hire joins the organization. These include setting up the workstation, setting up the computer and e-mail account, adding the new employee to payroll and benefits plans, briefing him or her on the employee handbook, arranging for the employee ID badge, and preparing uniforms and tools. The goal is to ensure you bring the individual up to speed instead of waiting for Day 1 to do all the logistical arrangements.

These are the easiest tasks that can be done quickly. However, we have seen some organizations where they do not prepare all of this upfront, and the employee ends up not doing any work even up to two weeks after they begin or only does relatively minimal work. As an organization, you lose productivity when new employees sit idle for longer than they should. It is worth noting that you ought to be mindful that new hires tend to be energized to start on their first day. Most often they experience mixed emotions such as being anxious, excited, happy, nervous, and blissful. Choose to leverage on those emotions to set them up for success from the first day onward!

Welcoming New Hires

Following is a simple practical example of how to welcome new employees to your organization. When you join a new group of friends, wouldn't you feel happy if they warmly welcomed you and included you in all their discussions and activities? The same applies when you join a family through a relationship or marriage. They welcome you into the family, and you feel great! Everyone loves to feel welcomed; it gives people a sense of belonging. This is exactly how a new employee would like to feel when joining a new organization!

Here is how you can make your soon-to-be employee feel welcomed:

- The hiring manager sends a welcome introductory e-mail and copies the team members with whom the candidate will be working. It would be awesome if you created a culture where you encourage your existing employees to send personalized welcome e-mails, so the new hire can build rapport with their coworkers right away.

- For employees whose nature of work does not require them to use e-mail, the above may not apply. For example, these employees could be skilled workers. You can still send a welcome message to them by phone. Be creative in how you word it. Or even send a visual welcome from the whole team!

Buddy Engagement: What Is It?

Another fantastic way to seamlessly onboard the new hire is engaging a buddy for the new hire. Who is this buddy? Ideally, it should be a high-performing team member, someone who aspires to learn, grow, and develop their networking and mentoring skills. You don't want to assign a buddy who has a negative mindset or is disengaged to the new hire!

Buddy engagement begins prior to the new hire's start date and continues for a certain length of time after he or she joins the organization. The duration of the buddy engagement can range from two weeks to four weeks, during which the buddy provides positive support to the new hire in the onboarding experience, ongoing learning, and network building.

Among the activities the buddy could help the new hire with are sharing experiences, explaining how things are done at the organization, answering questions, and referring him or her to other subject matter experts if the buddy is not able to provide the needed information. Buddies can connect the new hires to those who can support them in their roles.

Key Tip: The buddy should communicate with the new hire pertaining to how much time he or she will spend with the new hire on a daily basis so that the buddy does not get burned out.

Other Preboarding Activities

There are more exciting ways to preboard a new employee. You could schedule a lunch with the new hire, hiring manager, and the team members they'll work with. This creates an environment where they get to know each other in a casual setting and ease the anxiety of the new employee joining the organization.

If it is a remote working team, or if the new hire has not relocated yet, schedule a video call for the new hire with the hiring manager and team members. You can make it informal and fun by calling it virtual coffee/tea with "new hire name." It still gives everyone an opportunity to meet and greet.

Another warm approach to preboarding is to invite the new hire to your organization's social events that you might have, such as breakfast meetup, organization events, or social gatherings such as team dinners or team activities. We believe you are getting the idea! Happy exploring creative ways to preboard new hires.

Employee Onboarding and Engagement

On the new hire's first day of work, he or she is now officially your employee, and the onboarding process commences. It is important to ensure the employee experience is consistent from the preboarding process. The onboarding process will take anywhere between one and six months, depending on the nature of the job and your organization's culture. It is critical that you continuously engage your new employee as it is often during this period that the employee decides if he or she will stay with the organization. If the experience is not as per employee's initial expectation, you may find yourself looking for a replacement sooner rather than later. Staying engaged, monitoring the new employee's progress in the job, and following his or her assimilation into the company's culture are critical.

After acquiring the right talent, the employee experience is the next critical element in which the organization ought to continue investing its time, money, and effort in building a cohesive and engaged workplace.

IN CLOSING

We hope you found this book to be beneficial for you and your organization. Our intention is to provide tips that are easy to apply to your hiring lifecycle and result in acquiring the right talent for your organization.

We wish to thank you for reading our book. Our sincere hope is that some of what we've shared here moved you in a special way. If you'll now use some of these strategies to increase the quality of your hires, we would feel that we have achieved our intended objective of writing this book.

If you seek more information or clarification, please feel free to contact us. Here are our contact details:

✓ E-mail: TalentStrategist.APAC@gmail.com or enquiry@ acquiringtherighttalent.com
✓ Website: https://www.acquiringtherighttalent.com
✓ LinkedIn: https://www.linkedin.com/in/vilvaanthony/
✓ LinkedIn: https://www.linkedin.com/in/phyliswong/

We wish you all the best in your endeavors to acquire the right talents for your organization.

With much gratitude and appreciation, Vilva Anthony and Phylis Wong.

APPENDIX A

Talent-Planning Template

Organization Goals

Vision

Goals
Short, Medium, and Long-Term

Customers
Current and future customer landscape

Internal and External Impacts

Internal Factor Impact
Consider future growth or downsizing, process changes, and so on.

External Factor Impact
Consider industry trends, economic conditions, market shifts, and so on.

Outlook

Talent Needs
Skills and capabilities required to fulfill goals; noted areas of impact.

Current Talent Profile

Current Skills, Capabilities, and Capacity

Role Types and Quantities	Levels of Skills and Qualifications	Employment Types
Workforce role types with number breakdowns	Current workforce skills, competencies, and developmental goals	Employment types with full-time, part-time, contractor, internship, university hires

Current Talent Characteristics

Gender Distribution	Ethnicity Profile	Age Profile
Remuneration Profile (range)	Vacancy/Recruitment Practices	Exit Processes

SWOT Analysis

	Advantages	Disadvantages
	Strengths	**Weaknesses**
Current Consider current resources, capabilities, and performance strengths and issues. What is done well and what areas require improvement?		
	Opportunities	**Threats**
Future Identify potential opportunities and potential threats. What future developments could attract required talent? Are there potential skill shortages, talent competition, recruitment or retention issues to consider?		

Future Talent Profile

Future Skills, Capabilities, and Capacity

Role Types and Quantities	Levels of Skills and Qualifications	Employment Types
Workforce role types with number breakdowns	Future talent skills, competencies, and developmental goals	Employment types with full-time, part-time, contractor, internship, university hires

Future Talent Characteristics

Desired Gender Distribution	Ethnicity Profile	Ideal Age Profile
Desired Remuneration Profile (range)	Vacancy/Recruitment Practices	Exit Processes

Gap Analysis

Talent Needs	Gaps between State of Current and Future Talent	Priority	Measures to Take to Address Gaps
Role Types and Quantities			
Levels of Skills and Qualifications			
Employment Types			
Gender Distribution			
Ethnicity Profile			
Age Profile			
Remuneration Profile			
Vacancy/Recruitment Practices			
Exit Processes			

Talent-Planning Review and Evaluation

Date Completed	Completed By

Yes or No	
Is there a clear picture of where the business is going?	
Is there a strong understanding of future talent requirements?	
Have the areas of talent development need been identified in order to reach targeted goals?	

Successes Describe elements of the planning process that went well.	
Future Refinements Describe changes you would make to the process.	
Takeaways List key actions to bring forward future planning processes.	
Additional Comments	

APPENDIX B

Talent-Planning Leadership Questionnaires

For the Senior Leadership Team

Critical questions to ask leaders in an organization's talent-planning process.

1. How are customer demands expected to change (for example: increase, decrease, or shift in focus)?

2. How will technology change the way we work and interact with and deliver services to our customers?

3. Are we reorganizing the business? Are we creating or expanding business lines or services?

4. Are we eliminating or scaling back business lines or services?

5. Are we restructuring the work? Will workload distribution change?

6. Will work process improvements change the division of labor in the organization?

7. Will there be a new ratio of managers to employees?

8. Will there be a new balance of generalist and specialist roles?

9. Which current job functions and workforce competencies are critical to our mission and goals? Which will no longer be required in three to five years?

10. What new job functions and competencies will be required in three to five years?

APPENDIX C

Job Description Template

Employee:	Name
Position:	Sales Manager—Standard Product Division
Report To:	Name (Managing Director)
Direct Report(s):	Sales Standard Team: • Assistant Sales Manager • Sales Executives x 2 • Sales Executives x 2

Key Internal Departments to Collaborate with Closely for Success of the Role: Sales Operations/Support, Marketing, Production, Human Resources, Finance, and Senior Management.

Primary Job Purpose
Key person of overall sales division's achievements and leadership; proactive in ensuring sales targets, sales objectives, new market development, customer development, customer relationships, team development objectives are met; with the main aim to support the organization's (1) continued profitable growth, (2) diversification outside the current business segments and markets, (3) expansion of core competencies.

Roles and Responsibilities

Business Strategy
- Responsible for initiating research, market studies, SWOT analysis, and other relevant methodologies to support the effective development of short-term and long-term business strategies.
- Align sales department goals, processes, and resource allocation with business strategy.
- Present findings, projections, and recommended actions to senior management and other relevant team members.
- Plan, implement, and manage proposed recommendations and strategies/projects.
- Monitor and report on progresses proactively.
- Support and work closely with the relevant parties in decision-making processes.

Lead and Develop Teams
- Work closely with HR and senior management on sales team(s) talent planning, selection and hiring, onboarding, training and development, and team engagement.
- Propose, discuss, and execute team incentive/commission schemes that effectively drive the team in achieving the sales goals.
- Communicate team goals and all relevant information; identify areas for improvements in order to achieve the goals.
- Conduct performance feedback sessions regularly.
- Lead and drive team performance for achieving sales goals.
- Develop multiple sales teams.

Local Market Development

- Design and implement strategic business plan that expands company's customer base and ensures its strong presence.
- From the business strategy, determine annual sales objectives/targets and gross-profit goals with senior management.
- Achieve growth and hit sales objectives and targets by successfully leading and managing the sales team.
- Build and promote strong, long-lasting customer relationships by partnering with them and understanding their needs.
- Identify emerging markets and market shifts while being fully aware of new products and the competition landscape.
- Present sales, revenue and expenses reports, and realistic forecasts to the management team.

New Market Development

- Identify and secure relationships and sales opportunities with new overseas markets/customers by proactively undertaking a variety of sales activities, networking, and customer relationship development activities through online/mobile technologies and offline strategies in order to achieve sales targets and profitable objectives.
- Liaise with external resources and in-house teams to ensure support and deliverables and that activities are planned and completed effectively, achieve value for money and are of a high quality of work/service.
- Communicate proactively with key stakeholders, including the production department, to ensure delivery of quality results.
- Work closely with the marketing department to define the go-to-market strategy and target potential customers and partners.
- Collate and analyze market intelligence and prepare proposals for the strategies to senior management.
- Keep track of market performance; update proactively to the management.

- Grow and retain clients by continuously adding value to the clients in the form of, but not limited to, presenting new solutions and services.
- Ensure continuous effort and strategy in maintaining client relationships, achieving sales objectives, and market development.

Financial
- Monitor, analyze, report, and achieve the targets of division in terms of costs, revenues, margin, and cash in (collections).
- Responsible for the compliance of the company's accounting and finance procedures and policies in all aspects, including, but not limited to, the documentation, the approval process from the MD/other relevant PIC, client due diligence background check, and so on.

ISO Compliance
- Manage the effective workflow (planning, executing, reporting, and follow-up audits) to ensure compliance with the company's ISO standard.
- Educate and guide sales team on company's ISO workflow.
- Produce good-quality, accurate ISO reports for internal and external audits, with monthly reports to the managing director.

Supporting Role
- Cross-product division collaborations (for example, collaboration with the rental division).
- Support any company-related business events or exhibitions.

Others
- Compliance with all the company's published policies and procedures.
- Carry out ad-hoc business responsibilities from the managing director.
- Proactively arrange face-to-face discussions and updates with the managing director on a regular weekly or monthly basis.

Key Requirements
<ul><li>Sales-oriented, result-focused</li><li>Able to handle business projects and lead sales division independently</li><li>Good leadership and interpersonal skills in managing sales team for strong results</li><li>Proficient with the regulations of the local authority and other relevant compliances</li><li>Strong client engagement skills</li><li>High integrity</li><li>High team spirit and willingness to contribute</li><li>Committed and accountable</li><li>Innovative and able to generate practical solutions</li><li>More than six years of relevant working experience in relevant industries</li><li>Required language skill: English</li><li>Willingness to travel locally and abroad</li></ul>

Last Review and Update On:	Last Review and Update By:

APPENDIX D

Behavior and Competency Based Interview Questions

1. Tell me about a time in the last week when you've been satisfied, energized, and productive at work. What were you doing?

2. Tell me of the most aggressive goals you set for your area of responsibility. How did you achieve them?

3. Describe a time when you were asked to do something you had never done before. What did you learn?

4. Recall a time when you were assigned a task outside your job description. How did you handle the situation? What was the outcome?

5. Tell me about the time you provided a most effective intervention to a problem that the customer was facing. How was it received?

6. Tell me about a time that a customer was disappointed with your work. How did you respond?

7. Can you share an experience when a project dramatically shifted directions at the last minute? What did you do?

8. Describe the most significant change that you led or contributed to in your organization. What was the outcome?

9. Tell me about a time when you overcame the doubts of your team. What did you learn?

10. Give an example of when you had to work with someone who was difficult to get along with. How did you handle interactions with that person?

11. Tell me about the last time something significant didn't go according to plan at work. What was your role? What was the outcome?

12. Describe a situation where you needed to persuade someone to see things your way. What steps did you take? What were the results?

13. Tell me about a time when you had to juggle several projects at the same time. How did you organize your time? What was the result?

14. Have you ever had to "sell" an idea to your colleagues or business leaders? How did you do it? What were the results?

Tips to Getting the Desired Answers

1. Don't accept surface-level responses. When you ask for specific examples, make sure candidates don't give you only situational information. Here are some sample follow-up questions to probe candidates:

    a. Situation
        - What was the situation?
        - Why was it challenging/difficult?
        - Why was it necessary to change the process?

    b. Action
        - How did you come up with the idea?
        - What specifically did you do to champion and implement the improved process?
        - How did you involve others in implementing it?
        - What specific steps or actions did you take?

    c. Outcome
        - What was the outcome?
        - What was your customer's response to your approach?
        - What was the resulting impact of the solution on your business?
        - What knowledge/skills did you gain from it?

2. Give them time. Good answers often come after a moment of reflection, so don't rush candidates or write them off if they don't answer quickly.

ENDNOTES/CITATIONS

Introduction

1   Mason Stevenson, "Bad Hiring Costs—By the Numbers," *HR Exchange Network*, January 10, 2020, accessed April 26, 2021, https://www.hrexchangenetwork.com/hr-talent-acquisition/articles/poor-hiring-costs-by-the-numbers.

Chapter 1

2   Kendra Cherry, "Attitudes and Behavior in Psychology," *Verywell Mind*, February 20, 2021, accessed April 26, 2021, https://www.verywellmind.com/attitudes-how-they-form-change-shape-behavior-2795897.

3   "Candidate Experience in the Expectation Economy," *Resource Solutions*, 2020, accessed April 16, 2021, https://www.resourcesolutions.com/thought-leadership/candidate-experience-in-the-expectation-economy.html.

Chapter 5

4   Kristina Martic, "List of HR Statistics That Have Changed the Way We Recruit," *TalentLyft*, November 21, 2017, accessed April 26, 2021, https://www.talentlyft.com/en/blog/article/77/list-of-hr-statistics-that-have-changed-the-way-we-recruit.

5   "Global Recruiting Trends 2017—What you need to know about the state of talent acquisition," *LinkedIn Talent Solutions*, 2017.

Chapter 6

6   "The Future of Recruiting—How COVID-19 Is Transforming Hiring," *LinkedIn Talent Solutions*, 2020.

ABOUT THE AUTHORS

Vilva Anthony

Vilva is an Executive Leadership Coach, Career Coach, and Talent Strategist. She is dedicated to helping her clients become more effective in all aspects of their personal and professional lives. She assists her clients to discover meaning in their own lives and in their organization, which results in creating empowered individuals, a high-performance culture, an optimized and a productive workforce, and bottom-line enhanced organization performance.

Vilva has successful experiences coaching executives of all levels ranging from CEO, Managing Director, Vice President, Director, and Department Head to Individual Contributors and Teams. Her professional experience extends across an array of industries, including Information Technology, Advertising, Engineering, Retail, Food and Beverage, Training, and Nonprofit Organizations.

Prior to becoming a professional coach, Vilva was an accomplished HR Executive with extensive success over a career that spanned twenty-three years in the corporate sector. For about fifteen years she held HR leadership roles in Multinational Organizations. Her core expertise includes Talent Acquisition, Organizational Development, Talent/Leadership Development, and Compensation and Benefits. Vilva is an expert in the fields of leadership and organizational development, with a focus on the role of leaders in shaping high-performing cultures. Vilva has worked with senior leaders globally to design and deploy organizational transformation processes aimed at creating and sustaining effective large-scale change and driving business profitability.

Her credentials include a Master's Degree of Applied Psychology in Coaching and the globally recognized International Coach Federation (ICF) certification as a Professional Coach. She is also a certified coach with Marshall Goldsmith Stakeholder Centered Executive and Team Coaching. Additionally, she has a Master's Degree in Human Resource Management and Industrial Relations.

LinkedIn: https://www.linkedin.com/in/vilvaanthony/

Phylis Wong Sim Kuan

Phylis is an Entrepreneur, Executive Coach, a Talent Acquisition Adviser, and a passionate leader who walks the talk of "Inspire and Co-Create to Enrich Lives." Her clients include both organizations and individuals. She works with her clients in lifting the organization's and individuals' performances and achieving professional goals and personal purpose in life. Phylis believes and practices, "Everyone is potential in something, everyone deserves a chance to ignite his or her inner empowerment to enrich own live as well as lives of others."

Prior to founding her Talent Consultancy companies in 2012, Phylis had extensive experience in the areas of Headhunting, Talent Acquisition, Human Resources, Training and Talent Development, as well as leading operations and business units. She has served multinational companies in the industries of Luxury, Retail, Automotive, Banking, and Headhunting. She has successfully led two start-ups.

In her more than twenty years of working experience, Phylis has worked very closely with regional and senior leaders from various industries, including but not limiting to Retail, Luxury, FMCG, Manufacturing, Technology, and Hospitality to design and develop practical and sustainable strategies and programs in Talent Acquisition, Talent Development, and Talent Retention that drive business results.

Her formal credentials include a Bachelor's Degree in Business from the University of Strathclyde in Scotland, a Master's Degree in Applied Psychology in Coaching from HELP University in Malaysia, Certified Professional Coach from the Certified Coach Academy-International Coach Federation, Certified Executive Coach from Marshall Goldsmith SCC, and is a Certified Global Leadership Assessment (GLA360) practitioner.

LinkedIn: https://www.linkedin.com/in/phyliswong/

www.ingramcontent.com/pod-product-compliance
Lightning Source LLC
Chambersburg PA
CBHW021445210526
45463CB00002B/643